AKRON
FAMILY RECIPES

AKRON
FAMILY RECIPES

History and Traditions from
Sauerkraut Balls to Sweet Potato Pie

JUDY ORR JAMES

AMERICAN PALATE

Published by American Palate
A Division of The History Press
Charleston, SC
www.historypress.com

Copyright © 2022 by Judy Orr James
All rights reserved

First published 2022

Manufactured in the United States

ISBN 9781467152563

Library of Congress Control Number: 2022935411

For Jeff.

La vida buena.

CONTENTS

ACKNOWLEDGEMENTS

Wise words of encouragement from writer friends are posted above my desk. Akron historian Dave Lieberth's no-nonsense advice was "get your behind in the chair." Dear friend Ed Yeager suggested that I "shouldn't underestimate what a powerful personal journey this may be." I hadn't considered that. I embarked on this project with my librarian hat firmly in place. It would mean lots of research (my favorite thing) and talking to people about their family history—pretty much what I did for thirty-five-plus years. I wasn't expecting a personal journey, but indeed it was. I am exceedingly grateful to all of the wonderful folks I met along the way and for their incredible generosity and hospitality. I made lots of new friends.

I must thank my husband, Jeff James, for his tolerance and patience during this fun but challenging project, as well as countless neck rubs as I sat hunched over my laptop. Our daughter, Anna James, and her partner, Ryan Iwaszkiw, and son, Cary James, and his wife, Ashlee Moore James, have been supportive from the very beginning. My brother-in-law and former editor-in-chief of *Chemical & Engineering News*, Rudy Baum, agreed to "gently" edit my early draft. Thank you, dear Rudy. Many thanks to former *Akron Beacon Journal* food editors Katie Byard and Jane Snow. Katie's mention in her Akron Dish column and Jane's post on her blog, *See Jane Cook*, were a great help in spreading the word. I am grateful for their efforts over the years to celebrate and document Akron's food history. Former *Akron Beacon Journal* features editor Lynne Sherwin gave it the final polish with her keen eye and stellar editing skills. Many, many thanks to her.

Thank you to all who granted permission to include images from their collections, especially Leianne Neff Heppner, CEO of the Summit County Historical Society; Vic Fleischer, university archivist and head of Archives and Special Collections for the University of Akron; and *Akron Beacon Journal* editor Michael Shearer. A very special thank-you to the Akron–Summit County Public Library, especially Mary Plazo and the staff of Special Collections who work hard every day to preserve and share the history of our city. Amy Freels encouraged me to take this project on more than five years ago. Thank you, Amy.

Thank you to my former Akron–Summit County Public Library colleagues Iris Bolar and Carolyn Davidson Suddieth, who helped me to think about what to include and connected me with contributors for the African American chapter. The most valuable print resource I consulted was Dr. Shirla Robinson McClain's University of Akron doctoral dissertation, "The Contribution of Blacks in Akron: 1825–1975." The depth of her research is astounding. Other sources were Abel Bartley's 2004 Arcadia Publishing book, *Akron*; the 1940 edition of *Akron Negro Directory*; and Akron's only African American newspaper, *The Reporter.*

Sandy Clark and Anna Koenig of the German Family Society met with me as I began to work on my first chapter and suggested "must-include recipes" for the German chapter.

I am grateful for the gracious enthusiasm I encountered from Akron's Greek American community. Among the first I met were Chris Cherpas and his daughter, Maria Eliason. A special thanks to Chris for reviewing my essay. John Karipides provided useful information about the American Hellenic Educational Progressive Association (AHEPA) and referred me to George Nahmi, who filled in some gaps regarding the group's more recent history. I shared coffee one morning with Toula Detorakis Elefter and Noula Poleondakis Kountis, who helped me to learn more about the Pancretans. I would like to dedicate the Greek chapter to my dear friend Chryse Vernis Brown and her mother, Sophia Tzelissis Vernis. It was in their homes that I first tasted home-cooked Greek food. Sophia's homemade phyllo will forever remain a wonder to me.

Elizabeth Domotor was a gracious resource as I began my research for the Hungarian chapter. She clarified the various splits and mergers of Akron's Reformed Hungarian churches. Ralph Bormet and his cousin Fran McLaughlin shared a copy of their family cookbook, including many Hungarian family favorites. Thank you to Ron Easley and Sandra Bees Marr of the Akron Hungarian American Club for their help finding club photos.

It wasn't until I read Charlotte Marky's memoir, *Journey to Freedom* (Tate Publishing, 2015), that I fully understood the human toll of the Hungarian Revolution. Thank you to Miki Janosi, who offered some good tips and reviewed an early draft of this chapter. Jennifer Jacobs of Jacobs Heritage Farm introduced me to *The Streets Are Not Paved with Gold* by Terez D. Tibran (1961, Cleveland), a book that tells the stories of the Hungarian immigrant experience in northeast Ohio.

I am thankful to Marie Rizzo, president of the Margaret Judge Chapter of the Ancient Order of Hibernians. She spread the word to her group and offered suggestions about other folks to contact. Ann Jeffers, who has been a member for more than sixty-five years, graciously reviewed my chapter. Michael Namsick answered questions about the history of the St. Brendan Chapter of AOH, and Teresa Buck of MacConmara Dance Academy helped to clarify the history of Irish dancing in Akron. *Canal Fever* (Kent State University Press, 2009), edited by Lynn Metzger and Peg Bobel, illustrated by Chuck Ayers; and Mark J. Price's 2013 *Akron Beacon Journal* article about Hell's Half Acre were useful resources for learning more about Akron's early Irish.

A May 31, 1998 article in the *Akron Beacon Journal* provided a fascinating study of the Carovillese, who came from Krebs, Oklahoma, to Akron. Donna and Don Ferrante gave me a copy of the Sons of Italy cookbook, which is out of print. Mark Barbuto, president of the Italian American Societies of Summit County, arranged for me to speak to one of the group's meetings and supplied a list of local Italian clubs. Emma Dudones and her father, John, provided some good suggestions and leads for local Italian American food connections.

Helga Kaplan's 1979 Kent State University dissertation, "A Century of Adjustment: A History of the Akron Jewish Community, 1865–1975," was an invaluable resource for the Jewish chapter. *Jewish Life in Akron* (Arcadia Publishing, 2005) by Beverly Magilavy Rose and Arlene Cohen Rossen was an especially useful reference for information about the social and family life of Akron Jews. A heartfelt thank-you to Beverly, who connected me with several folks and their recipes and reviewed an early draft of my essay.

Mary Beth (Dombrosky) Grether, former kitchen manager for Akron's Polish American Citizens Club, was a generous resource. She adapted several club recipes for home use and reviewed an early draft of my essay. Many thanks to Stan Olesky for his input and knowledge about local Polish-owned food businesses and for reviewing my draft.

My first Serbian connection was Anita Ondreyka, one of the bake sale organizers for St. Archangel Michael Serbian Orthodox Church. She referred me to Slavica Djosanovic, who encouraged her fellow church ladies to share their recipes. She also served as my liaison with the church board, which reviewed my essay and helped me understand the complicated history of Serbs. St. Demetrius Serbian Orthodox Church Parish president Milorad Jovich also reviewed the Serbian chapter and donated a copy of the church's 1997 history, a valuable reference. Ron Koltnow's well-researched and delightful account of the history of Serbian fried chicken, *Barberton Fried Chicken: An Ohio Original* (The History Press, 2018), was a useful starting point for learning about Summit County's early Serbs and their food traditions.

My very first West Virginia contact was Heather Zinn Anderson, who met with me and shared her copy of *Our Family Recipes: Old and New*, published by Akron's West Virginia Society. Tom Jones's books *On a Burning Deck*, volumes 1 and 2, are outstanding and important contributions to the history of Akron's rubber industry and the fine folks who came here to make it great. Other invaluable published sources include Mari-Lynn Evans's book *The Appalachians* and Steve Love and David Giffels's *Wheels of Fortune.* Much useful information was gleaned from Susan Allyn Johnson's 2006 Ohio State University doctoral dissertation, "Industrial Voyagers: A Case Study of Appalachian Migration to Akron, Ohio, 1900–1940." "Akron: Standing Room Only!" by Edward Mott Wooley, published in the July 1917 issue of *McClure's* magazine, offered a journalist's view of the city written at the time.

I am grateful to those who have told the sauerkraut ball story before me. Former *Akron Beacon Journal* journalist and food blogger Jane Snow was the first person I consulted. Her well-researched and entertaining newspaper articles about sauerkraut balls were my starting point, and she kindly read one of my first drafts. Details about Gruber's Restaurant were shared by William Gruber, grandson of the founder, Max, and son of Max's son Roman. Rick Vogel supplied information about his father, Richard "Dick" Vogel, who once worked for Gruber's, later taking his talents to Marcel's Restaurant in Cuyahoga Falls. Anita Schreibman and her grandfather John Simonetti shared the recipe for television chef Lorenzo Simonetti's version. Parris Girves, son of Brown Derby founder Gus Girves, was a gracious resource, sharing the restaurant's current and delicious recipe for sauerkraut balls. Yvonne DiCarlo Clemens, daughter of Brown Derby chef Don DiCarlo, valiantly searched for the original Brown Derby recipe. Although she was unable to locate it, she confirmed that it was almost identical to Gruber's recipe. Thank you to Marilyn McCafferty for finding the Brown Derby recipe shared with *Akron Beacon Journal* readers. The Bunny B story could not have been told without the help of family members of K.T. Salem, who first produced them commercially. Earl Hatfield and Kathleen Salem filled in many blanks and confirmed that Bunny Bidinger was, indeed, Bunny B. Pete Rizopulos, who purchased Bunny B in the 1990s, clarifying details about the later years before the company was bought by Ascot Valley Foods. I am especially grateful to Dave Lieberth for tracking down the "original" Bunny B recipe, thereby solving the mystery of Bunny's identity.

The History Press team, especially acquisitions editor John Rodrigue and production editor Abigail Fleming, were a pleasure to work with. I am thankful for their patience, responsiveness and expertise.

Finally, my deepest gratitude goes to the folks who so generously shared their Akron family stories and recipes.

INTRODUCTION

When I was growing up in the 1960s, my mother owned three cookbooks: *Betty Crocker's Picture Cookbook, Better Homes and Gardens New Cookbook* and *The General Cooks*, published by the Women's Auxiliary of Akron General Hospital. On a shelf next to them was her battered recipe box overstuffed with recipes she had clipped from the *Akron Beacon Journal* and various women's magazines, most of which she never made. Although a wonderful mother, she wasn't much of a cook, and unlike my father, who loved to eat, food meant little to her. There were certain dishes she made well, and she was very proud of her "martini stew," maybe the closest she came to gourmet cooking. With the exception of spaghetti and the occasional La Choy Chow Mein from a can, ethnic foods never graced our family dinner table.

Although three of my four grandmothers were of German ancestry, I don't recall that they made anything that was especially ethnic. Any German dishes we ate were usually enjoyed at the German social clubs Liedertafel and Mannerchor. I was very young at the time and don't remember much about the food, however. What impressed me most was Mannerchor's cool bowling machine that occupied the kids while the adults enjoyed their pre-dinner beer and cocktails. The first real pizza we tasted was made by Jennie Simonetti, a vibrant Italian lady who took care of us when my parents went away. Mrs. Simonetti was well into her seventies at the time, less than five feet tall, and had more energy than all four of us put together. She arrived with a bag of apples and turnips to cook for herself but always treated us to huge pans of lasagna and thick, cheesy pizza, made with her own sauce, of course. It was a revelation. By the time I was a teen, my friends and I had discovered the wonders of carryout pizza, usually from Gino's on Copley Road, and inexpensive Italian fare at Parasson's, as well as Chinese food at Pagoda Garden located in Fairlawn Plaza. I was highly motivated to reproduce these exotic dishes and learned that I could make some of them at home with the help of cookbooks I checked out from the Akron Public Library. Ingredients for Italian food were readily available at the Acme (I had not yet discovered DeVitis), and Dragon Trading Company, a tiny Chinese grocery on Frank Boulevard (later on Dopler Avenue), was my source for items like fresh bean sprouts and egg roll wrappers.

My love of food and family is matched by my love for our great city and its rich history. When I shared this project idea with my daughter, Anna, her response was, "Mom, if you don't do this, who will? These are your three favorite things: food, family history and local history." She was right. I am food-obsessed; I worked as a genealogy librarian for years and have been fascinated by our city's history since Mrs. McKinnon's fourth-grade class at Erie Island, where we studied the history of Akron. Suddenly, history was fun and meaningful, and I looked at our city with new eyes knowing that my ancestors lived, worked, farmed, shopped and worshipped here, some as early as the 1820s.

When I was hired in 2001 by the Akron–Summit County Public Library to create a new department at Main Library devoted to genealogy and local history, I had lots of ideas about what I thought our young department should focus on. One that consistently rose to the top was preserving the history of Akron's cultural and ethnic groups. In 2015, we collaborated with local historian Sharon Moreland Myers to create a display featuring Akron restaurants of yesteryear. Sharon's father, Charles Marcellus Moreland, co-owned Marcel's restaurant, one of Akron's long-established "white tablecloth" restaurants. An *Akron Beacon Journal* article about our project helped to spread the word, and soon we were inundated with menus, matchbooks, barware and other memorabilia, including a charred whiskey bottle, a survivor of the 1979 fire that destroyed Martini's on Copley Road. In the fall of 2015, we hosted an opening reception for everyone who loaned or donated materials for the display, mostly folks whose families owned restaurants. Hugs, tears and memories were shared. How did Kaase's make those potato baskets for its famous creamed chicken? How about that flaming shish-kebab served by turban-festooned waiters at Yanko's? How I miss Sanginiti's lasagna. As I listened to these stories, I realized how deeply woven our food history is into our community's history and, sadly, how many treasured restaurant and family recipes have been lost. How many of us wish we had asked Aunt Betty to write down the chicken paprikash recipe that existed only in her head? How many of us have our own recipes that no one else in the family could replicate once we are gone? Although my mother-in-law, Mary Alice James, never wrote down her fried chicken recipe, she taught my sister-in-law Jennell Woodard how to make it. She is now the expert and treats us once or twice a year to "Nama's" fried chicken. It's a gift and reminder of what Mary Alice was to our family.

My original, and admittedly naïve, vision was to create a cookbook that would include stories and recipes from all of Akron's ethnic and cultural groups, including our newest immigrants. It didn't take long for me to realize that such an undertaking would be impossible. But, how to narrow it down? German, Italian and Polish for sure, but what about Russian, Ukrainian, Lebanese and even Swedish? Yes, Akron had a small but thriving Swedish community. Narrowing the chapters by population numbers seemed to be the most logical approach. Still, it was hard to leave out some of the groups that have contributed to Akron's rich and diverse food history. My apologies if your chapter is not included.

"You honor my family." I will never forget these words of gratitude spoken by Angelo DeVitis when I interviewed him in 2000 for an oral history project to document Akron's neighborhoods. Over the course of an hour, he shared the history of his family and its iconic North Akron food business. He was not alone. Almost everyone we spoke with shared memories of neighborhood markets, bakeries, restaurants and memorable family meals and recipes, many of which have been lost. Like old photographs, family recipes connect us to our past and are gifts and treasures to be preserved. If you are the keeper of your family's precious recipes, please be sure to write them down and share them with your children and grandchildren. In the meantime, I hope that the *Akron Family Recipes* cookbook contributes in some small way to preserving and celebrating Akron's family food traditions. I hope I have honored your families.

AFRICAN AMERICAN

Located in the progressive and abolitionist Western Reserve, Akron was a relatively welcoming community for early Black residents who made our city home. It was a stop on the Underground Railroad, the town where abolitionist John Brown would establish and run his business and where Sojourner Truth gave her famous "Ain't I a Woman?" speech at the Women's Rights Convention of 1851. In 1830, only 5 free Black people were living in what was then Portage Township. Although a few were skilled tradesmen, working as canal boatmen, blacksmiths and masons, most of the early Black settlers worked as laborers. By the 1860s, Akron's Black community also included preachers and skilled laborers such as tailors, hairdressers and barbers. From the end of the Civil War through the 1920s, the population increased dramatically as thousands left the South for greater opportunities in the North. In 1916, the *Akron Beacon Journal* reported that more than 1,500 "negroes" had moved to Akron from the South and that Akron was now home to a Black doctor, an attorney was "expected to arrive soon" and several restaurants were Black-owned.

While their employment and living conditions had improved by then, it was also a time when restaurants, pools and hotels were segregated, and Black patrons were required to sit in the balconies of local theaters. Lack of housing for all newcomers was a problem, especially for Black people faced with finding landlords who would rent or sell to them. This was also the era of the rise of the Ku Klux Klan in Akron. In the 1920s, the local chapter boasted a membership of fifty thousand, including a majority of the school board and several elected officials.

When the 1930s and the Great Depression brought unemployment to Akron, the city's Black residents were hit hard—usually the first to be laid off and the last to be hired. This era saw the rise of clubs and agencies devoted to addressing Black social and educational needs. In 1931, First Congregational Church hosted a race relations conference where problems such as housing, employment, education and youth were discussed. "Negro Youth in the World Tomorrow" was the theme of a weeklong conference sponsored by Wesley Temple AME and the Association for Community Colored Work. An outgrowth of the Colored YMCA, it was the forerunner of the Akron Community Service Center and Urban League, now known as the Akron Urban League. The 1940s and 1950s saw some improvement in conditions for Black citizens with greater numbers employed by the rubber industry, as well as in retail and professional jobs. Progress was made toward better housing conditions with the creation of Akron's first public housing projects developed under the Akron Metropolitan Housing Authority, established in 1938.

The 1960s and the civil rights era brought more changes to Akron and its Black community. The Akron branch of the NAACP sent a sizable delegation to the 1963 March on Washington. Akron's first Head Start centers were established in 1965 as a collaboration between churches, community centers and the Community Action Center. The year 1968 was pivotal and tumultuous for the country, and Akron was not immune; the city was rocked by unrest and rioting on Wooster Avenue and Arlington Street. In 1993, the *Akron Beacon Journal* won a Pulitzer Prize for "A Question of Color," its yearlong study of race relations, and President Bill Clinton selected Akron as the site of his first town hall meeting for his initiative on race. The University of Akron continues this tradition today with "Rethinking Race," a yearly forum to address issues of race in our city.

WHERE THEY LIVED

Akron's earliest Black residents lived north of downtown around North Broadway, North High and Furnace Streets, mostly in old and dilapidated housing. Although the majority worked as laborers, some started small businesses to serve the neighborhoods where they lived. By the 1930s, North Howard Street had become the center of commerce for Akron's Black community, and for years, it was known as "Akron's Harlem." It was where you shopped, dined, went to the barber, visited the dentist and relaxed on the weekend at one of the jazz clubs. It was also the only place where Black visitors could find a hotel where they were welcomed, even if you were Cab Calloway and performing at the Palace Theater that night. The best known was the Matthews Hotel, owned by businessman George Mathews. Other hotels listed in Akron's 1940 *Negro Directory* included the Garden City, Plymouth, Hotel Exchange and the Green Turtle, which had a restaurant and tavern. The Ritz Theater on North Howard was the city's only nonsegregated movie theater at the time. In addition to regular movie fare, it also offered live shows featuring famous acts like Moms Mabley, B.B. King, Della Reese and John Lee Hooker. In 1939, Cleveland's Black newspaper, *Call and Post*, held elections to select a "mayor of North Howard Street," with the winner receiving a prize of twenty-five dollars.

Although many Black workers were making better wages by the 1930s, good housing was elusive, and Black citizens were segregated. Akron practiced "redlining," and neighborhoods with the highest percentages of Black households were always rated as the highest risk for investment. As the city's Black population doubled in size between 1940 and 1950, some people moved into other neighborhoods, including Tobin Heights and Wellington Heights in East Akron. Wellington Heights was marketed in a 1945 *Akron Beacon Journal* real estate advertisement as a new and low-cost development for "coloreds." African Americans also moved into areas around Arlington Street, Wooster Avenue and the east side of Summit Lake. Urban renewal projects of the 1960s and 1970s had an enormous effect on Akron's Black community, effectively wiping out entire urban neighborhoods and forcing them into other parts of the city. Since the 1970s, Akron's neighborhoods have become increasingly integrated, with African Americans living in all sections of the city.

CHURCH LIFE

Church served as more than a place of worship for Akron's early Black community. Like the benevolent societies established by Akron's immigrants, church was a place for support, education and advocacy. Akron's first Black church, Zion AME (now Wesley Temple AME Zion), was formed in 1866. Like most early churches, it was started by a group that met in private homes or rental halls. Shiloh Baptist was Akron's first

Mount Olive Baptist Church choir members. First located at the corner of West Bartges and Coburn Streets, the congregation dedicated a new building on Slosson Street in 1967. The church and its pastors were involved in the civil rights movement. *Opie Evans Papers, The University of Akron, University Libraries, Archives and Special Collections.*

Black Baptist church, founded about 1877. Established by a former slave, the congregation first met in a hall on South Howard Street. It is now known as Second Baptist Church. Within the next three decades, others would follow, including Roberts Street Church of God (now Arlington Church of God), Greater Bethel Baptist, Mount Olive Baptist, another Shiloh Baptist, Mount Zion Baptist, Centenary Methodist (now Centenary United Methodist), Antioch Baptist and Bethel AME (now St. Paul AME). As Akron's African American population grew during the mid-twentieth century, more congregations were established throughout the city, and while some occupy large and impressive buildings, many still exist in small storefronts throughout Akron's Black neighborhoods.

CLUBS AND ORGANIZATIONS

In addition to churches, clubs and fraternal organizations offered Akron's Black citizens additional opportunities for camaraderie and social activism. Because white organizations did not allow African Americans to join, some joined "colored" chapters of established white groups such as the Knights of Pythias, Masons, Oddfellows and the Elks. The Grand Order of True Reformers was an exclusively Black national organization established in Virginia after the Civil War; its Akron Chapter was founded in 1899. In 1935, the Negro 25 Year Club was formed and, within a year, was planning and fundraising to rededicate the John Brown monument, which still stands today in Perkins Park. As the economic stature of African Americans improved, clubs for professional men and business owners were formed, including the Negro Business League (1920) and Akron Frontiers International (1938). Since 1960, the Eta Tau Lambda Chapter of Alpha Phi Alpha fraternity has served our community through its nonprofit housing corporation, Alpha Phi Alpha Homes Inc.

Officials of Akron's Black Shriners, Al-Kaf Temple 109, and auxiliary, Al-Kaf Daughters of Isis Court 144, at the auxiliary's annual ball in 1964. Photograph by Horace Stewart. *Opie Evans Papers, The University of Akron, University Libraries, Archives and Special Collections.*

The Hampton Miracle Singers tea held at the Negro Women's Council Home on Wooster Avenue included a fashion show and talk by Helen Arnold, president of the Akron Chapter of the NAACP. 1963. *Opie Evans Papers, The University of Akron, University Libraries, Archives and Special Collections.*

As early as the 1880s, Akron's Black women were meeting and socializing in groups. Although some were auxiliaries of men's groups, many were formed independently. The Daughters of Jerusalem, established in 1885, was one of the earliest and most exclusive women's clubs. Dozens of groups formed, and although most were social in nature, some focused their efforts on bettering life for Black people in Akron. There were so many women's groups that the Council of Negro Women was created in 1932 to foster collaboration among twenty-two neighborhood block clubs. The Tea Time Study Club was formed in 1942 by social activist Bertha Moore for Black democratic women. She named it after the Boston Tea Party because, as she put it, "We were revolutionaries." Black professional women had their own group, the Negro Business and Professional Women's Club, chartered in 1965. Among the most active women's groups today are the Akron Alumnae Chapter of Delta Sigma Theta, the Zeta Theta Omega chapter of Alpha Kappa Alpha and the Akron chapter of Jack and Jill of America.

RESTAURANTS AND FOOD BUSINESSES

Whether at the family dinner table, a church supper, a community festival or restaurants, the food traditions of Akron's African American community are celebrated every day. Because Akron's early Black residents weren't welcomed at most dining establishments in the city, they established their own taverns and restaurants. One of the earliest Black restaurant owners was entrepreneur, sometime bootlegger and crime boss Kurt Brown, who operated a restaurant on North Howard Street in the 1920s. Until the 1970s, North Howard Street was the dining and entertainment hub for Akron's Black community. Soul food restaurants would later pop up throughout the city, where some of the best barbecue and other traditional southern dishes could be found. Porter's Soul Food Restaurant on Copley Road and Arnold's Baroudi on Brown Street were popular in the 1970s. The Arnold family later owned Arnold's Rib House on East Cuyahoga Falls Avenue until it closed in 2009. Queen's Barbecue and Shrimp on Copley Road was operated

The Bonanza Restaurant, 461 Chittenden Street. Specializing in barbecue ribs, chicken and short orders, its slogan was "the gold mine of good eating." It was designed and built by Willie Horton and his wife, Dorothea. 1963. *Opie Evans Papers, The University of Akron, University Libraries, Archives and Special Collections.*

Photographer Opie Evans was also an entrepreneur. His mobile concession stand dubbed the "Dreamboat" parked outside of the Diamond Super Market on South Howard Street. *Opie Evans Papers, The University of Akron, University Libraries, Archives and Special Collections.*

for nearly ten years by Queen Walker. One of the most successful was the Smoke Pit, established in 1968 by Matthew Ebeneezer, with locations on North Howard, South Maple and South Arlington. Barbecue Boss on Copley Road, owned by brothers Leroy and Ray Singletary, was known for its award-winning sauce. Southern and soul food traditions are celebrated today by LA Soul, Edgar's, K&D Kitchen and Nicole's Southern Kitchen.

Pride, perseverance, church and family have defined Akron's Black community since the first African Americans came to Akron in the 1830s. In spite of harsh living conditions and discrimination, they rose up. Working together through their churches, clubs and social service agencies, they made life better for themselves, their children and our community.

Enjoy!

Dorothy O. Jackson

Dorothy O. Jackson was born in Akron in 1933, not long after her parents, William and Dueallie of Oklahoma, moved to Akron, where her father took a job with Goodyear. For years, she was the family caregiver until taking jobs with Goodwill, Akron Metropolitan Housing and the City of Akron, where she served under two mayors as deputy mayor for intergovernmental relations. A fierce advocate for people with disabilities, Dorothy was a sought-after sign language interpreter, signing for countless community events. In 1982, she wrote *How to Boil Water and Other Things Too Good to Miss*, a cookbook for a young man she thought she would marry. Having every intention of continuing to work after their marriage, she did not want to be the only cook in the family. The preface includes a poem written by Dorothy about love and cherishing those who are close to us. It closes with these wise words: "Don't do what fools do and let it casually slip beyond your reach and plummet from careless fingertips. Hold to the happiness you have and cling to it and cherish it, lest taking it for granted you let it slowly perish."

Bisquick Chicken

Assorted chicken parts (drumsticks, thighs, wings, breasts and back)
Salt
Pepper
Lemon pepper
Crushed red pepper flakes
Bisquick
1 or 2 leeks, sliced, white part only
1 medium onion, sliced
4 cloves garlic, sliced

Wash chicken and season with salt, pepper, lemon pepper and crushed red pepper. Place Bisquick in a paper bag and dredge chicken parts.

Place leeks, onions and garlic in the bottom of a roasting pan. Add 2 inches of water. Place chicken on top of vegetables. Cover and bake at 350 degrees until done, about 45 minutes to 1 hour, basting occasionally with broth.

Doris (Smith) Porter

Born in 1930 in Sylacauga, Alabama, Doris came to Akron with her husband, Samuel Porter. She was a dynamic wife, mother, leader and business owner. In the late 1970s, she partnered with Samuel to establish Porter's Soul Food Restaurant on Copley Road in the heart of West Akron. Doris served as the lead chef while preparing comforting soul food. The operation of the restaurant was truly a family affair, as Doris's six children could be found assisting to ensure that her soulful creations were devoured by hungry customers. The restaurant was a hit in the community and frequented by a variety of locals, including former NBA player Gus Johnson. Doris passed away in 2006 and left no record of her cherished recipes; however, her daughter, Alesia Smoot, observed her mother over the years and mastered many of them, including this favorite for cornbread dressing with smoked turkey and gravy. The Porter family hopes that these recipes bring joy to your family as the savory aromas fill your home. May you find comfort and cook with love as you prepare Doris's soul food creations. *Contributed by Doris's granddaughter Ebony Porter.*

Cornbread Dressing with Smoked Turkey Leg and Gravy

Turkey Leg
1 smoked turkey leg
Salt, pepper, garlic powder and garlic salt

Cornbread
2 cups all-purpose or self-rising flour
2 cups cornmeal
½ teaspoon baking powder
½ teaspoon salt
⅓ cup vegetable oil
2 eggs, beaten
1 cup whole milk

Dressing
1 green bell pepper, chopped
1 small onion, chopped
2 stalks celery, chopped

3 tablespoons dried sage
2 eggs, beaten

Gravy

To be poured over the baked dressing. The key is to use a cast-iron skillet and cook it on high heat.

⅓ cup vegetable oil
½ cup flour
1 teaspoon Lawry's seasoned salt
1 teaspoon garlic powder
1 teaspoon garlic salt
1 teaspoon pepper
1 small onion, chopped
1 cup lukewarm water

Boil turkey leg in about 4 cups of water. Add seasonings to taste and simmer on medium heat for about 2 hours or until meat falls off the bones. Add water as needed to create a broth. Reserve broth and cut turkey into bite-size pieces.

Mix cornbread ingredients together in a large bowl. Bake in a greased pan (a cast-iron skillet works best) at 350 degrees for 55 minutes until golden brown. Let cool. Crumble and place in a large oiled roasting pan or casserole dish. Add green pepper, onion, celery, sage, reserved broth and turkey to crumbled cornbread. Taste and adjust seasonings. Add beaten eggs. Bake at 350 degrees for 1 hour, until golden brown. Overcooking will dry out the dressing.

While dressing is baking, make the gravy. Heat oil in a skillet and add flour. Stir with a wire whisk on high for about 5 minutes. It will look clumpy, but keep stirring until oil is absorbed and it turns brown. Add seasonings and onion and stir. Gradually add water and keep stirring until smooth. Let simmer on medium heat for 20 to 30 minutes, adding more water, if needed. Adjust seasonings to taste. Serve with cornbread.

Dasha Smitherman

A recent graduate of the University of Akron's hospitality program, Dasha is a chef who dreams of one day owning her own food truck and, someday, a restaurant. In 1965, Dasha's grandmother Martha L. (Sykes) Price; aunt Martha J. (Sykes) Hamilton; father, Robert L. Jackson; and uncles Clifton White II and Willie Bob Cunning of Columbus, Mississippi, moved to Akron seeking jobs and better schools. Her grandmother and grandfather Ralph and Vivian Smitherman came from Selma, Alabama, to Akron and had three children: Beverly (Smitherman) Whelchel; Dasha's mother, Varetta Smitherman; and Anthony Smitherman. Ten years ago, Dasha's aunt Martha asked her to make three large pans of macaroni and cheese for Thanksgiving dinner. It was such a success that she is now the designated maker for all family holidays. According to Dasha, "Once you mess up the mac and cheese, you're not allowed to make it anymore." Every family's recipe is a little different, and although Dasha has her own chef-inspired riff on the traditional recipe, her family prefers this old-school baked version. Dasha is proud to be the official macaroni and cheese maker and loves knowing how much her recipe is enjoyed by her family. Her hope is that this recipe is passed down to future generations.

Baked Macaroni and Cheese

2 pounds elbow macaroni
¼ pound salted butter
½ to ¾ gallon whole milk (amount is determined by the depth of your baking dish; ingredients should fill at least halfway up the dish)
1 (12-ounce) can evaporated milk
2 cups shredded sharp Cheddar cheese
2 cups shredded Colby Jack cheese
1 tablespoon garlic powder
1 tablespoon white pepper
Salt

Preheat oven to 350 degrees. Bring 4–6 quarts of generously salted water to a boil. Cook macaroni until al dente. In another pot, melt butter over medium heat. Do not burn the butter. Add the whole milk and evaporated milk. Cook over medium-high heat until it starts to bubble.

Do not allow it to scorch. Stir in cheeses and whisk until smooth and melted. Add garlic powder, white pepper and salt to taste. Turn off heat. Drain macaroni and stir into sauce. Pour into 2 greased 9x11 baking dishes and bake for 30 to 40 minutes until it is brown and bubbly.

Tena (Jones) Price

In the 1930s, Ulysses Simpson Price of Clanton, Alabama, came to Akron, where his first job was laying bricks on Howard Street. Soon he would join the ranks at Firestone Tire and Rubber Company and marry WPA seamstress Tena Jones, with whom he raised five children. After retiring from Firestone in the mid-1940s, he and Tena opened Case Lunch at 103½ Case Avenue, where they served workers from Goodyear and Firestone until selling the business around 1976. It was known for Tena's homestyle southern cooking, especially fried chicken, ribs, sweet potatoes and black-eyed peas. Case Lunch was one of the earliest and longest-surviving Black-owned restaurants in Akron. *Submitted by Tena's daughter Aria (Price) Campbell.*

Mama Price's Cabbage

1 head cabbage
3 to 4 tablespoons olive oil
Salt and pepper
1 green pepper, sliced
1 red pepper, sliced
1 yellow pepper, sliced
1 onion, sliced
Garlic, optional
Cayenne pepper, optional

Wash cabbage, keeping the dark green leaves. Cut into four sections and shave each section into thin slices, including dark green leaves. Over medium heat, add olive oil and one cup of water to skillet. Add dark green slices of cabbage first and let them begin to cook. Add remaining cabbage and salt and pepper to taste. Let cabbage cook down. Add peppers and onions. Cook for about 20 minutes. Do not overcook. If you like garlic, add that. If you like spicy, add cayenne pepper.

Royal Arnold

Royal Arnold learned to cook at the feet of his North Carolina–born grandmother Lydia Crandall and his mother, longtime Akron Public Schools board member and community activist Helen Crandall Arnold. In 1969, Royal and his mother opened Arnold's Baroudi, a cocktail lounge and restaurant specializing in soul food and live weekend entertainment. It was named in honor of his mother's brother, middleweight boxer Sammy (Baroudi) Crandall, who died in the ring in 1948. Royal and his wife, Marian (Hinton), later operated Arnold's Rib House on East Cuyahoga Falls Avenue, which featured their famous barbecue, as well as chicken, catfish and walleye. This baked bean recipe, served at both of his restaurants, makes enough to feed a crowd.

Arnold's Baked Beans

2 (117-ounce) cans baked beans, drained and rinsed
1 ¼ cups finely chopped green bell peppers
1 ¼ cups finely chopped red bell peppers
1 large onion, finely chopped
½ bag brown sugar
2 cups tomato paste

Mix all ingredients. Place in large baking dish. Bake uncovered at 400 degrees for about 45 minutes or until bubbly on top.

Dorothy (Bright) Bolar

A native of Brentwood, Tennessee, our mother primarily made Angel Biscuits for Easter and Christmas dinners—when baked ham was served. Later in the evening or on the following day, we used the leftover biscuits to make ham and biscuit sandwiches. These southern biscuits include yeast to make them lighter than usual biscuits. Several versions were found in our family files, but mom's measurement adjustments and the staining on the handwritten paper prove that this recipe version was used multiple times.
Contributed by Dorothy's daughters, Iris and Carmen Bolar.

Angel Biscuits

5 cups flour
1 teaspoon baking soda
2 teaspoons baking powder
1 teaspoon salt
½ cup sugar
1 cup shortening, cut up fine
2 packages dry yeast
2 cups buttermilk
Melted butter or margarine (for dipping before baking)

In a large bowl, mix all dry ingredients. With fingers, rub in shortening pieces to get coarse crumbs. In a medium bowl, dissolve the yeast in ¼ cup of warm water for 5 minutes. Add the buttermilk to the dissolved yeast and mix. Add the liquid mixture to the dry ingredients and mix well. Cover with a kitchen towel and allow to stand 1 to 2 hours in a warm place. Preheat oven to 400 degrees. Lightly knead the dough five times on the counter using a very small amount of flour to prevent sticking. Roll or press the soft dough to ½ inch thick. Cut biscuits. Dip each biscuit into melted butter and place in baking pan(s) lined with parchment. Bake for 15 minutes.

Marie (Ford) Campbell

Marie was a young bride in the 1940s when she and her husband, Luther, came from Mississippi to Akron, where he was employed by B.F. Goodrich for thirty years and she was kept busy raising their eleven children. According to her daughter Sherrylon, they always ate well, and her mother did her best to please everyone's tastes. "There was so much love and we always ate— Mom was an excellent cook, mother, grandmother and person." In spite of her busy home life, Marie found time for her church, St. John CME, where she was an active member of the Carver Chapter of American War Mothers. Marie loved to bake, and her pound cake was a family favorite often served for Sunday dinner or for company. Mostly, it was served plain, but sometimes, as a special treat, with ice cream. *Contributed by Marie's daughter Sherrylon (Campbell) Adams.*

Mama Campbell's Pound Cake

1 pound butter or margarine, softened
1 (1-pound) box confectioners' sugar
6 eggs
2 cups cake flour
Dash salt
2 teaspoons vanilla extract
1 teaspoon lemon extract (other extract flavors may be substituted according to your taste)

Cream butter until smooth. Add sugar, blending until light and fluffy. Alternate adding eggs and flour to creamed mixture. Add salt and extract. Pour into well-greased and floured tube pan. Bake at 350 degrees for 1 hour.

Donzella Michele (Malone) Anuszkiewicz

According to Donzella, sweet potato pie is a classic African American dessert, and no winter holiday is complete without it.

> *You would be hard-pressed to find an African American family that doesn't know how to make it. Everyone's sweet potato pie tastes different, and each pie will taste different than the last one they made—but everyone knows how it is supposed to look and taste. In our culture, if one runs across a bad-tasting pie at a holiday gathering, the rumor will spread rapidly because to bake one is a rite of passage that one is forbidden to mess up.*

After moving out on her own, Donzella made more than one attempt to make a sweet potato pie for a Thanksgiving dinner to which she was invited. It just wasn't right. "The sweet potatoes were always too loose, and it wasn't worthy of presentation at the dinner table!" A frantic and tearful Thanksgiving Eve call to her mother solved the problem. Donzella had been baking rather than boiling the sweet potatoes. Since then, her pies have always been perfect. This recipe is dedicated to Donzella's mother, Veralene (Harris) Malone, daughter of Donzella Mae King, and granddaughter of Sallie Mae Murphy-Barnes, affectionately known as "Granny." Granny was born in Alabama in 1894 and lived to be 101 years old, surviving her two children, three husbands and six boyfriends. As a young bride, Sallie first moved to Portsmouth, Ohio, and then to Akron. There was always something good to eat in her kitchen, including sweet potato pie.

Sweet Potato Pie

Recipe note: All ingredients are to taste and based on the size of the sweet potatoes—this is why no two pies taste the same. The unused batter may be frozen for another pie or used as a dessert without a pie shell.

2 deep-dish unbaked pie crusts (homemade or store-bought)
2 or 3 large sweet potatoes boiled with skin on until tender enough to mash
1 to 2 sticks salted butter (Use more for a richer pie, or if your sweet potatoes are very large. Donzella uses 2 sticks.)
2 to 3 teaspoons allspice
2 to 3 teaspoons nutmeg
2 eggs
1 to 2 (14-ounce) cans sweetened condensed milk
½ to 1 cup granulated sugar
½ to 1 cup brown sugar
Lemon extract (optional, use sparingly)

Peel warm potatoes. Add the butter and mash together with a potato masher. Potatoes should be warm enough to melt the butter. Scrape buttered mashed potatoes into a large mixing bowl. Add spices. Add eggs and condensed milk while the mixer is operating. Start with 1 can and add more for extra sweetness. Add ½ cup each of granulated and brown sugars. If more sweetness is desired, add more to taste. Do not add too much granulated sugar, as it will make the filling too thin. If it is too loose, add another egg and additional flour, a little at a time. Mix batter until smooth and all strings are removed from the batter—they usually end up between the mixer blades. If desired, add lemon extract to taste. Pour batter into pie shells. Bake at 350 degrees for 20 to 30 minutes or until the crust is brown, the filling is no longer loose and a toothpick comes out clean.

GERMAN

If you lived in Akron's Goosetown during the late 1800s or early 1900s, you didn't have to speak English or leave your neighborhood for your daily needs. Most of your neighbors and local merchants spoke German, the native language of many who lived in the area around Grant Street and Wolf Ledge. Even the factories where you worked were likely owned and operated by German Americans. Your church offered services in your home language, and your children were taught German at school.

One of the largest groups of immigrants to settle in Akron, German Americans have made a lasting mark on our city. The earliest to arrive were men who came in the 1820s to work on the Ohio and Erie Canal after finishing the Erie Canal in New York. The greatest influx, however, came during the second half of the nineteenth century and early twentieth, a time when many European immigrants came to our shores. The Germans came for a variety of reasons, but thousands came to escape persecution after the 1848 Revolution. Many worked as laborers, tradesmen and merchants, and some, including men like "Oatmeal King" Ferdinand Schumacher and printer and publisher Paul E. Werner, became leaders of industries that reached beyond Akron.

WHERE THEY LIVED

Most German immigrants settled in Goosetown, the Grant Street neighborhood that was home not only to Germans but also immigrants from other eastern European countries. The nickname Goosetown was bestowed because it was said that many of the residents kept geese in their yards. A close-knit community with its own shops, taverns and groceries, it even had its own German-language newspapers, *Germania* and *Columbia*.

CHURCH LIFE

Church was an important anchor of family and community life for Akron's German Americans. Established in 1854, Zion Lutheran Church was the first to serve the Protestant German population. St. Bernard's, established in 1861, was home to German Roman Catholics. The current church building was constructed in 1905 on land purchased with funds donated by King Louis of Bavaria. Akron's German Methodists started their church in 1886, meeting at Akron's First Methodist until they dedicated their own building at the corner of Grant and Pearl Streets. Not all German immigrants were Christian, of course. The founding members of Akron's first Jewish congregation in 1865 were German immigrants.

CLUBS AND ORGANIZATIONS

To support their fellow immigrants, Akron's early Germans established benevolent societies to help the newly arrived assimilate into their new country. These groups and clubs also served as gathering places for social events where old-world traditions, especially music, were celebrated and preserved. Akron's first German club was the Akron Liedertafel (singing society), established in 1855. A saengerbund, or choral society, it met in various locations throughout the city, including the German Hall, later known as the Music Hall, at the corner of Exchange and High Streets, and the Kaiser Hall on South Main. The Liedertafel took part in many German music and singing festivals (saengerfests) held throughout the country. In 1925, the club dedicated its own building on Carroll Street, where it operated until 1965, when it was razed for construction of the interstate. Although the club building was a victim of urban renewal, its members continued to meet at the German Beneficial Union until the late 1970s. The Liedertafel was one of many German groups.

The Akron City Directory lists twenty-four "German Societies" in its 1925 club listings—some were associated with a region in Germany, while others were political or had a specific focus such as singing or athletics. They included the German Club, founded by Akron publisher Paul Werner and undertaker George Billow, Mannerchor, Sons of Herman, Turner Club and the German American Club. These groups were highly social, sponsoring concerts and festivals throughout the year, including German Day, an annual picnic co-sponsored by multiple German clubs. These daylong celebrations attracted thousands who came to dance, eat, sing and celebrate all things German. Proud Americans, their picnics often included patriotic parades and displays. An account published in the August 5, 1939 edition of the *Akron Beacon Journal* stated, "Most of all, the festival is a demonstration of their allegiance…to the land of their adoption. It is necessary to emphasize this because of the tendency among the ill-informed to fail to distinguish between the German people and their temporary political leaders." Many of Akron's German Americans served proudly in the military from the Civil War on.

Over the decades, most of these clubs dissolved. Their membership aged, and interest in the old ways declined as younger people felt less connected to their German roots. Some that held on as social clubs opened memberships to those of non-German background. One of the last to close, the Liedertafel, was a popular lunch spot for downtown workers, politicians, lawyers and other movers and shakers until the building was razed in 1965. Another that held on for years was the German American Club located on Grant Street. Established in 1911 as the German-Hungarian Singing Society, the doors on its 1928 building were permanently shut in 1997.

Keeping German traditions alive today are the Akron Turner Club, Sons and Daughters of Herman and the German Family Society. Devoted to maintaining physical and mental discipline, the original Turner Clubs or Turnverein offered gymnastics and fitness classes to members in a Turnhalle, or gymnasium. The Akron building, located on Grant Street in the heart of Goosetown, was built in 1888. Although demolished in 1975 to make way for urban renewal, the Turner Club remains active

The German American Club on Grant Street served Akron's German Americans from 1928 to 1997. *Akron–Summit County Public Library.*

Members of the German Family Society youth dance group perform at the 1978 grand opening of the club's new home, Donau Park in Brimfield. *Akron Beacon Journal Collection, Summit Memory, Akron–Summit County Public Library.*

today at its location in Tallmadge. Founded in 1895, Sons of Herman, now Sons and Daughters of Herman, was located on East South Street until 1991, when they moved to their current location on the second floor of the Hungarian American Club. Many of the founding and current members of the German Family Society identify as Donauschwaben or Danube Swabians, ethnic Germans who lived in various countries of southeastern Europe, including Yugoslavia and Hungary.

The aftermath of World War II saw the expulsion and displacement of thousands of Donauschwaben from their homes, resulting in a wave of German immigrants to the United States, mostly after 1950. Those who came to Akron established the St. Bernard's German Club, which met at the downtown church until 1960. As the club grew and required more space, it entered into an agreement to use the German American Club building on Grant Street. That arrangement worked well for a few years, but soon the newer and younger club's energy and focus on family activities didn't mesh with the established club's goals. Within a few years, members were looking for their own building. In 1973, they purchased a building and sixteen beautiful acres in Brimfield, Ohio, known as Donau Park. Their emphasis on family and community has paid off. Now known as the German Family Society, it is a thriving organization with something for everyone. Its calendar of events includes traditional celebrations such as Oktoberfest, Traubenfest (Grape Fest), Maifest (Mother's Day) and Fasching (Mardi Gras), as well as Lenten fish fries, dances and concerts. Several club groups are devoted to keeping children and teens involved in the community, and the ladies' auxiliary, Frauengruppe, is strong and active, organizing many of the club's social events, especially those involving food and cooking.

RESTAURANTS AND FOOD BUSINESSES

As Akron's German population grew, its cultural influence extended beyond Goosetown and its clubs. Germans owned groceries, bakeries, taverns, restaurants and breweries throughout the city. Akron's Germans were beer lovers and operated scores of breweries, including the Burkhardt, Renner and Akron Brewing companies. Opened in 1901 by Albert Buehrle and Louis Dettling, the Rathskeller was a favorite Main Street watering hole and restaurant for more than thirty years. In 1914, the Black Whale Inn managed by Eugene Gruhler advertised its "German kitchen" and imported pilsners on draft. Gruhler later managed the Liedertafel, served as chef for the Old Heidelberg and, in the 1930s, ran his own place in Highland Square, the Romany, which featured "gypsy music." John Kraker opened the popular Old Heidelberg in 1934 in the former site of the Rathskeller. Kraker outfitted the restaurant with the Student Prince bar, a decorative bar manufactured by the Liquid Carbonic Corporation in Cleveland and exhibited at the 1933–34 Chicago World's Fair. Later eateries serving German fare were Henry Wahner's Lamplight on North Main Street and the Bavarian Haus on East Market. The Lamplight served German and Hungarian food at its location on North Main starting in the late 1960s until it moved to Kent in 1979. Until it closed in 1994 after thirty-five years, the Bavarian Haus was known for its traditional German, Austrian, Hungarian and Yugoslavian foods, live polka music and an "authentic Bavarian atmosphere," according to 1970s advertisements in the *Akron Beacon Journal*.

With the exception of some members of the German Family Society, few Akronites can claim to be 100 percent German anymore. All of us,

Henry Feuchter Grocery. The son of German immigrants, Henry Feuchter and his father, John, established this East Exchange Street store in 1869. *Summit County Historical Society of Akron, Ohio.*

Known as Schroeder's, the Buckeye Cafe was owned by German immigrant Charles Schroeder. He later built a twenty-room hotel and bar on the property. Pictured here circa 1890s. *Akron Beacon Journal Collection, Summit Memory, Akron–Summit County Public Library.*

German immigrants Charles Wilhelm and Jacob Brodt operated a meatpacking company on South Main Street. Wilhelm later co-founded the Akron Cracker Company, which was sold in 1892 to National Biscuit. 1880. *Akron Beacon Journal Collection, Summit Memory, Akron Summit County Public Library.*

however, can be proud of what these industrious and inventive immigrants brought to our city: hard work, industry, pride, patriotism, food, music and, of course, beer.

Guten Appetit!

Beverly (Moll) Sensius

Although Beverly's paternal grandparents were German immigrants, she didn't learn to cook German dishes until marrying her husband, George, a German born in Yugoslavia. Following World War II, George's family left Yugoslavia and moved to Austria, where he grew up. In 1956, when George was nineteen, he and his mother, Maria, came to Akron, where his brother, aunt and cousin were already living. Maria taught Beverly to make all of the traditional German recipes loved by George, including sauerbraten, which is traditionally served on Christmas Eve. Beverly and George are active members of the German Family Society.

Sauerbraten

Beef brisket, approximately 4 pounds
1 cup vinegar
3 cups water
1 tablespoon salt
1 medium onion, sliced
3 tablespoons pickling spice
1 carrot, sliced
2½ tablespoons vegetable shortening
¼ cup sugar
⅓ cup flour
2 gingersnap cookies, crushed
½ cup red wine

Place brisket in a large bowl or casserole dish. Mix vinegar, water, salt, onion, spices and carrot. Pour mixture over meat and cover. Let meat brine for 3–4 days, turning several times.

Drain meat and wipe dry, reserving brine for gravy.

Grease roasting pan or Dutch oven with the shortening. Heat on stovetop and sear the meat on both sides. Add ½ of the reserved brine and cover tightly. Roast at 300 degrees for 2 hours, occasionally basting the meat. When the meat is almost done, sprinkle the sugar on the meat. Roast an additional 5–10 minutes, turning the meat until the sugar is dissolved.

Thicken the remaining brine with the flour and crushed gingersnaps. Pour over meat. Cover and roast at 300 degrees for 30 minutes. Remove meat and stir wine into gravy.

Elizabeth (Zimmer) Bormet

Both of Ralph Bormet's parents were immigrants of German ethnicity and Austro-Hungarian citizenship. His mother, Elizabeth, came with her parents to the United States in 1908, when she was just three years old. Ralph's father, Jacob, came as a boy to Akron with his mother, Julia, and his father, Antony, who had saved enough money while working in a New York City meatpacking plant earlier to return with his family and move to Akron. With Antony's experience as a meat-cutter and Julia's baking skills, they would open, over their lifetime, five restaurants in Akron. The most successful was the Grant & South Restaurant and Dining Hall located on the streetcar line between Goodyear and Firestone, where it did a booming lunch and dinner business. When Elizabeth and Jacob married in 1923, Elizabeth took a job at the restaurant, where she worked until it closed in the late 1920s. About that time, Jacob and Elizabeth opened their restaurant, the Rose Villa, on South Main Street. Ralph's extended family worked together to compile their favorite family recipes, including some from the Bormet family restaurants. *Contributed by Elizabeth's son Ralph Bormet.*

Stuffed Cabbage Rolls

1 good-sized head cabbage (not too solid)
1 pound ground beef
½ pound ground pork
1 onion, chopped
1 teaspoon salt
½ teaspoon pepper
2 teaspoons paprika
¼ cup uncooked rice
1 egg, well-beaten
1 (28-ounce) can sauerkraut

Remove the outer leaves of cabbage and remove the core. Place cabbage in a large kettle of boiling water. Boil for about 2 minutes or until leaves are wilted. Remove the leaves, one by one. Continue placing cabbage back into the kettle, removing leaves as they become wilted. Repeat as often as necessary until all leaves big enough to hold stuffing are off. Shred the remaining cabbage and set aside.

Mix the beef, pork, onion, salt, pepper, paprika, rice and egg. Take a cabbage leaf and cut off the back rib, being careful not to cut through the rib. Place 2 tablespoons of meat mixture on each leaf. Start to roll on rib end, tuck in sides, and finish rolling. Use all the cabbage leaves big enough to stuff. Drain sauerkraut and reserve juice. Place half of the sauerkraut and shredded cabbage in the bottom of a kettle or Dutch oven. Place cabbage rolls on top and cover with remaining sauerkraut and cabbage. Add just enough water to cover the top of rolls. Cover the pot and cook over low heat for 2 hours. If it is not sour enough, add some of the saved sauerkraut juice.

Sylvia (Opperman) Andrews

This family favorite was created by Sylvia's German grandmother Elizabeth Opperman of Raufelhausen, Germany. Sylvia's mother, Marie Opperman Coles, brought this recipe to the United States when she immigrated in 1962. When Sylvia married in 1975, Marie passed it on to her daughter. It has been adapted for American ingredients and products.

Rinderrouladen (Rouladen)

2 pounds beef braciole or round steak, sliced or pounded to ¼-inch thickness
2 large onions, sliced
Cooked bacon, 1 slice per roll
Whole dill pickles, sliced lengthwise to ¼-inch thickness (one slice for each roll)
Hard-boiled eggs, ½ per roll
⅓ cup butter
¼ cup flour
2 beef bouillon cubes
Salt and pepper

Cut beef slices into 3-inch-wide strips. Sauté onion in a little oil until tender. Place bacon, onions, pickle slices and egg on each filet. Form into a roll and secure with string or toothpicks.

In a large skillet, heat butter over medium heat. Add beef rolls and cook until brown on all sides. Remove rolls and set aside. Add flour to the pan and stir to make a roux. Add 2 cups water and bouillon cubes. Place beef rolls into gravy, cover and cook over low heat for about 1 hour. Season to taste with salt and pepper.

Theresa (Holetz) Sensius

Theresa Holetz was born in the former Yugoslavia, now Croatia. During World War II, her family was driven out of their home and, after many difficulties and hardships, ended up in a camp in Austria. After seven years of hoping to return to their home, the family decided to move to the United States, first living in Texas and, in 1953, moving to Akron. Theresa completed her education in Akron and was married in 1959 to Joe Sensius, who immigrated in 1955, also from what is now Croatia. From 1978 to 2002, Joe and two partners operated a successful machine shop. Theresa and Joe, along with their children and grandchildren, are active members of the German Family Society. They enjoy passing along the customs and traditions of their heritage to younger generations in the hope that they will do the same. Faschiertes is a recipe that has been enjoyed by generations throughout Europe. Theresa describes it as "peasant food—simple, good and hearty, something that one could fix quickly after a day of working in the fields." Although there are countless variations of faschiertes, the cook used whatever meat was available. Because Theresa's family raised pigs, theirs were made of pork. She likes to serve them with mashed potatoes and a creamed vegetable like green beans, peas or spinach.

Faschiertes

1 pound ground pork
¼ cup finely chopped onion
⅓ cup plain bread crumbs
A little water or milk to keep the meat moist
Salt and pepper
Flour for dipping
Vegetable oil for frying

Mix pork, onions, bread crumbs, water or milk and salt and pepper. Form into four or five patties or mini-loafs. Do not make them too thick, or the centers won't cook. Dip each patty or mini-loaf into flour, coating all sides. Heat oil in a pan and fry on medium to medium-high heat until bottoms are nicely browned. Turn and brown the other side. Variations: You may also use a combination of ground meats and an egg. If you prefer, day-old bread soaked in milk or water can replace the bread crumbs; additional milk or water may not be necessary. A variety of seasonings such as garlic, sweet or hot paprika or Italian seasonings may be added for flavor.

Anna Koenig

The daughter of German parents, Anna was born in Yugoslavia. During World War II, the family was captured by Yugoslav partisans and placed in a concentration camp for more than three years. She came to the United States as a newlywed in 1957 with her husband, Friedrich "Fritz." A coal miner, Fritz wanted to find a better life for himself and Anna. Anna had an aunt in Akron who encouraged them to come here, and Monsignor Wolf at St. Bernard's helped to facilitate their immigration. Anna is an active member of the German Family Society, helping to oversee the kitchen and serving as the cultural director. She has taught German cooking classes and works with the youth groups, teaching them traditional songs and poems.

Spaetzle

2 eggs
½ cup milk
1 ½ cups flour
½ teaspoon salt
2 to 3 tablespoons butter

Fill large pot ⅔ full of water. Add 1 teaspoon salt per quart of water. Bring to a boil. Reduce heat to slow, gentle boil. Beat eggs and milk with a fork. Combine flour and salt and add to egg and milk mixture. Stir with a wooden spoon until the flour is blended and the mixture is smooth. Using a spaetzle maker, add dough mixture to boiling water. Cook until spaetzle rise to the top. Test to make sure they are fully cooked. When cooked through, drain thoroughly in a colander and quickly rinse with cold water. Continue to drain, shaking colander to dry as much as possible. Melt butter in a saucepan. Add spaetzle, browning them to your taste.

Frances (Stefan) McLaughlin

Frances "Fran" McLaughlin's father, Frank Stefan, was born to Nick and Apollonia (Evelyn) Stefan at 800 Carnegie Avenue in a house rented from the Young family, owners of Young's Hotel. In 1912, Nick and Apollonia came from Austria-Hungary to Akron and worked for the Youngs. The family moved to a house closer to Nesmith Lake, where Fran was born. She has fond memories of swimming and boating in the canal and Nesmith Lake with her four siblings. Her grandmother told her that she was not permitted to get married until she learned to make homemade noodles. Although she didn't learn to make noodles before marrying her husband, David, she and other family members compiled a family cookbook dedicated to the cooks in her family. It includes many traditional German recipes from the Stefan, Bormet and Zimmer families.

German-Style Spinach

2 (10-ounce) packages frozen, chopped spinach
6 strips bacon
2 tablespoons flour
2 cups milk
¼ teaspoon salt
Pinch white pepper
1 tablespoon finely chopped onion

Cook spinach according to package directions. Drain and squeeze dry. Fry bacon until crisp; reserve drippings. Crumble bacon and set aside. Add flour to bacon drippings and blend over low heat. Slowly add milk, stirring constantly until sauce is smooth. Add salt, pepper and onion. Add cooked spinach to the cream sauce. Simmer slowly until thickened, about 10 minutes. Top with bacon.

Sandy Clark

As a young woman, Sandy Clark toured Germany with her mother. During their visit, Sandy met two young ladies from the Boston area, and the three became fast friends. Vowing to return, Sandy joined them for a second trip and decided to stay. She lived there for a little more than two years working at various jobs. One of her traveling pals married a German boy and stayed in Germany. It was there that Sandy met her husband, a young GI named Tom Clark. They were married in 1970 and moved to Suffield, Tom's hometown. Although Sandy is unsure if she has German roots, she has a deep fondness for German heritage and is an active member of the German Family Society, serving as the public-relations director. When her daughter was married and held her reception at the club, Sandy was astounded to see two long tables laden with homemade German cookies and pastries made by members, a club tradition. Sandy got this recipe from a coworker when she was working for a German hotel.

Chocolate Apricot Bars

Dough
3 cups flour
1 cup butter
3 tablespoons sugar
2 egg yolks
1 teaspoon baking powder
1 teaspoon grated lemon rind
6 tablespoons whole milk

Filling
2½ cups ground walnuts
1 cup sugar
1 (10- or 12-ounce) jar apricot preserves

Icing
6 squares semisweet baking chocolate
4 tablespoons whole milk
4 tablespoons sugar
¼ cup butter

Mix dough ingredients until no lumps remain. Divide dough into three balls of equal size. Mix nuts with sugar and set aside. Roll out each dough ball until approximately 15x10 inches. Place one sheet onto 15x10 baking pan, stretching dough to edges. Spread one-half of preserves over dough. Sprinkle half of nut and sugar mixture over preserves. Place another sheet on top of the mixture. Spread with remaining preserves and nut and sugar mixture. Cover with the remaining sheet of dough, making sure that edges are tight to prevent preserves from burning. Bake at 350 degrees for 25 minutes. Let cool completely before topping with icing.

Place chocolate, milk and sugar in a double boiler. Cook over low heat until smooth and creamy. Add butter and stir until the mixture is spreading consistency. Spread over cooled bars. When icing is completely cool, cut into bars.

Liz (Freimuth) Miller

This traditional and beloved strudel is a family favorite made by Liz's mother, who brings it to every holiday gathering and family function. It is so coveted that family members are known to cut and hide large portions, ensuring that they have some to take home. Liz and her family are active members of the German Family Society.

Mom's Stretch Strudel Dough and Fillings

Dough
4 cups flour
1 egg
1 teaspoon salt
4 tablespoons warm vegetable oil or melted butter
¼ to ½ cup water

Place flour on board or counter and make a well. Add egg, salt, 2 tablespoons oil or butter and ¼ cup of water. Using fingertips to knead, work in enough water to make a soft dough. Brush dough with remaining oil or butter. Cover with plastic wrap and let sit at room temperature for 30 minutes.

Sprinkle tablecloth or other cotton cloth with a small amount of flour. Stretch the dough until it is about 12 inches square and ⅛ inch thick. Place hands close together with palms down and quickly place them under the dough. Gently lift and stretch dough by moving hands apart until dough is almost paper-thin. Lay dough on floured cloth. Using fingertips, continue pulling dough until it is paper-thin.

Follow directions for spreading the filling. Tear off thick edges of dough. Lift edge of cloth and roll as for a jelly roll. Place seam side down on baking sheet greased with warm vegetable oil. Trim ends and tuck under to seal. Sprinkle 1 tablespoon warm vegetable oil on top. Bake at 350 to 375 degrees for 30 to 45 minutes until brown.

Cottage Cheese Filling
1 (16-ounce) container large-curd cottage cheese
4 tablespoons sugar, divided
1 egg
½ teaspoon cinnamon, or more if desired
⅓ cup farina
3 tablespoons warm vegetable oil or melted butter

Combine cottage cheese, 3 tablespoons sugar, egg and cinnamon. Drop onto the stretched dough. Sprinkle with farina, warm oil or melted butter and remaining tablespoon of sugar.

Apple Filling
4 cups peeled and sliced apples
½ cup sugar
⅓ to ½ cup dry bread crumbs
¼ to ½ teaspoon cinnamon
3 tablespoons warm vegetable oil

Toss apple slices with sugar. Spread mixture over prepared dough. Sprinkle with bread crumbs, cinnamon and oil.

Elizabeth (Ulrich) Armbrust

Elizabeth and her parents, Frank and Rufina, came to the United States in 1956 from Nuremberg, Germany. A young woman when she arrived, Elizabeth found work as a housekeeper for an Akron family, later taking a job in a restaurant located at Five Points, where the owner discovered her talent for baking. In addition to waiting on customers, she supplied cakes and pastries for the restaurant. Her parents worked for Sacred Heart of

Jesus Catholic Church on Voris Street, where they lived in an apartment. They cooked for weddings, parties and the Knights of Columbus meetings, where their culinary talents were recognized by the leader, who ordered their baked goods for his family and friends. Her father's co-workers at Goodyear placed orders, too. Soon the Ulriches needed to buy larger equipment to fill these orders, which the Knights of Columbus leader picked up at seven o'clock each morning. This was the beginning of the Ulrich Bakery on Grant Street, where Elizabeth made a different type of strudel each day. The bakery never advertised and didn't even have a sign. Word of mouth was enough to spread the word about their delicious baked goods. When Elizabeth's father became ill in 1970, the bakery closed. Although the family moved to Suffield, they continued to fill special orders for their favorite customers.

Nut Sticks

Nut Mixture
2 pounds ground walnuts
9 heaping tablespoons graham crackers, crushed, plus additional
for assembling cookies
9 egg whites from extra-large eggs
1 scant tablespoon vinegar
1 (32-ounce) bag confectioners' sugar

Topping
4 egg whites
1 scant tablespoon vinegar
1 ½ cups confectioners' sugar

Nut mixture: In a medium bowl, combine walnuts and graham crackers. Set aside. At high speed, beat egg whites until stiff, adding vinegar while beating. Beat in confectioners' sugar. Gradually fold nut and graham cracker mixture into egg white mixture. Refrigerate for 1 hour.

Topping: Beat egg whites until stiff, adding vinegar while beating. Slowly add confectioners' sugar and mix until firm. Cover bowl and set aside.

Grease 2 baking sheets with a very thin film of shortening. Flour baking sheets, shaking off excess. Spread a layer of crushed graham crackers on baking board or waxed paper in a 4-inch-wide strip. Place one-fourth of nut mixture on the end of the graham cracker strips and roll into the graham crackers. Roll and pat to form a long slab about ½ inch tall and 2 inches wide. Repeat with the remaining nut mixture, making four strips.

Spread ¼ of the topping mixture on each slab, taking care not to let mixture drip over the sides. Using a non-serrated knife and small spatula, cut cookies into 1-inch strips; after cutting with a knife, slide spatula under the cookie until it hits the knife. Tilt spatula back and angle knife away to pull the cookie away. For a clean cut, wipe the knife clean after each cut. Place cookies on greased baking sheets and place sheets on oven rack positioned one notch below the center.

Bake at 325 degrees for 20–25 minutes, turning pans after 10 minutes. Bake until the cookie topping just begins to turn a tan color.

Marcia Sines

Born in Wertheim and raised in Wurzburg, Germany, Marcia came to the United States in 1971 and married Donald Sines, an American citizen. Although not a family recipe, almond spritz is a traditional German cookie. According to Marcia, cookies are not the popular sweet snack that they are here in the United States. In Germany, cookies are traditionally reserved for weddings and high holy days like Christmas and Easter. A member of the German Family Society, Marcia is a regular volunteer for the club's annual Oktoberfest and helps out with weddings, when needed.

Almond Spritz Cookies

¾ cup sugar
½ cup blanched almonds
1 ¾ cups flour
¾ cup butter, cut up
¼ teaspoon almond extract
1 large egg

In food processor with knife blade attached, blend sugar with almonds until almonds are very finely ground. Add flour and remaining ingredients. Pulse just until the dough pulls away from the side of the bowl. Following the manufacturer's directions, pack the dough into a cookie press. With choice of disk inserted, press dough onto an ungreased large cookie sheet, placing cookies 2 inches apart.

Bake cookies at 350 degrees for 12 to 14 minutes until lightly browned around the edges. Transfer cookies to wire rack to cool completely. Repeat with remaining dough. Store in a tightly covered container for up to 2 weeks. Makes 4½ dozen cookies.

Judy (Ruff) Saccogna

Judy Saccogna's father, William Ruff, was the son of William and Louise Ruff, both of whom emigrated from Germany to Pennsylvania as children. After marrying, William and Louise moved to Akron, where William, a butcher, operated Ruff's Meat Market in downtown's City Market from about 1907 until his death in 1928. Judy often made dishes her father remembered from his childhood, especially bonasalat (wax bean salad), crumb cake and lebkuchen. She discovered this lebkuchen recipe in the *Akron Beacon Journal* and made it for him every Christmas until he passed away in 1996. She misplaced the recipe but found it in 2015. Much to her delight, "I baked a tray at Christmas and my taste buds were requited! My family members were not big fans, but when I eat a piece, I think of my dad who WAS a big fan."

Daddy's Lebkuchen

2¾ cups flour
1 teaspoon baking powder
1 teaspoon baking soda
2 teaspoons ground cinnamon
½ teaspoon ground cloves
1½ teaspoons ground cardamom
1¼ cups sugar
¾ cup honey
2 tablespoons water
2 eggs
¼ cup orange juice

1 (12-ounce) package semisweet chocolate chips or 4 ounces German chocolate,
shaved
1 cup walnuts, chopped
½ cup mixed candied fruit, chopped
Sifted confectioners' sugar

Sift together the flour, baking powder, soda, cinnamon, cloves and cardamom. Set aside. Combine sugar, honey and water in a 2-quart saucepan. Bring to a boil, stirring occasionally over medium heat. Remove from heat and pour into a large mixing bowl. Cool to room temperature.

Add eggs and orange juice to sugar and honey mixture. Beat with an electric mixer at medium speed for 1 minute. Add dry ingredients and beat at medium speed for 2 minutes. Stir in chocolate, nuts and candied fruit.

Spread batter in greased 9x15 jelly roll pan. Bake at 325 degrees for 35 minutes until it tests done with a toothpick. Cool and store covered for 3 days to develop flavor. Dust with confectioners' sugar and cut into squares.

Delight (Rinner) Beezley

Delight grew up in a German-Swiss-Mennonite family on a farm in Iowa, where she spoke German until she went to kindergarten. A graduate of Iowa Wesleyan College, she taught home economics in Iowa for two years, followed by a job with the Farm Security Administration. She married chemist and fellow Iowan Lawrence Beezley in 1942. Shortly after their marriage, Lawrence accepted a position with B.F. Goodrich in Akron. They eventually settled in Green Township, where they raised their three children: Elizabeth, Lawrence and Dana. This recipe is adapted from a Mennonite cookbook. Delight's daughter Dana has fond memories of making Knee Patches with her mother and recalled that her Iowa relatives, who preferred them salted rather than sugared, stored them in a large stoneware crock. They are called Knee Patches because the baker would stretch the dough across her knee to make it as thin as possible. *Submitted by Delight's daughter Dana Beezley-Kwasnicka.*

Knee Patches

4 cups flour
½ teaspoon salt
3 eggs
1 cup heavy cream
Vegetable oil for frying
Confectioners' or granulated sugar

In a medium bowl, sift flour and salt together. Beat eggs in a separate bowl and add cream. Stir flour mixture into the egg mixture to make a soft dough. Pinch off and roll enough dough to make a ball about the size of a large marble. Roll out each ball until as thin as possible or, as the Swiss do, cover your knee with a tea towel and stretch the dough over your knee until very thin. Deep fry in 375-degree oil until a delicate brown. Drain on paper towels and dust with confectioners' or granulated sugar.

GREEK

Greeks were later immigrants to Summit County, the greatest number arriving between 1910 and 1920. Most were young, single men who came with the intention of working, making money and returning to their homeland. Many, especially those who did not speak English, worked as laborers, including dozens of young men who lived and worked in Goodyear's construction camp alongside other immigrants hired to build factory buildings for the booming company. Others became entrepreneurs, starting businesses such as shoeshine stands, fruit stores and confectioneries.

Where They Lived

Most of Akron's early Greek immigrants settled around North Howard Street, an area sometimes referred to as "Greek Street" or "Little Greece." By 1920, North Howard Street was home to business owners with the names Economou, Spanopoulos, Athenos, Tundoukas, Demopoulos, Pappas, Topougis, Lukaris and Syracopoulos. Among the earliest businesses were coffeehouses where men could share news from home and discuss Greek politics, especially the conflicts taking place in their home country. By the 1930s, a number of Greek families were living in East Akron, many living in boardinghouses on East Market Street and others in the neighborhoods near South Martha Avenue.

CHURCH LIFE

Church is the spiritual, cultural and social heart of Akron's Greek community. Although they didn't have a place of worship for many years, Akron's early Greeks were devout, meeting in various rooms and halls until they were able to raise funds to build their own church. The newly formed congregation discovered that fundraising wasn't easy. Many members were young bachelors who, according to the 1967 church history, "were accustomed to the way churches were run in their villages where the priest's livelihood came from his small fields, the contributions of his parishioners being only a few coins collected every Sunday." The church trustees were undeterred, making regular Sunday collection visits to Greek-owned coffeehouses, fruit stands and restaurants. In 1916, Annunciation Greek Orthodox Church was chartered by the Holy Synod of the Church of Greece.

All was well until 1922, when the congregation suspended its services due to political differences among members during the Greco-Turkish War, some pledging their allegiance to King Constantine and others supporting Eleftherios Venizelos. They would soon come together and move forward with their dream of building a church. Under the leadership of Father Kapenekas, who arrived in 1926, the congregation strengthened its efforts and in 1928 purchased property on Union Street. Despite the Depression, construction began, and the new church was dedicated in November 1930.

As the congregation grew, so did the need for classrooms and a larger community hall. In October 1963, the new Hellenic Cultural Center was dedicated. Since 1958, the church has hosted an annual Greek Festival where all things Greek are celebrated, especially food made by an army of volunteer cooks and traditional dancing by youth groups. The church's Thursday gyro luncheons are popular with downtown workers, and its annual Easter Bake Sale, "the biggest bake sale in town," sells thousands of traditional pastries and hundreds of loaves of braided Easter bread each year.

CLUBS AND ORGANIZATIONS

Tightknit and proud, Akron's Greeks were intent on improving their status in the community. In 1923, the Good Friendship Association was formed; its purpose was to help new arrivals assimilate and to raise the image of Greeks in Akron. Soon they merged with the newly established American

The Akron chapter of the American Hellenic Educational Progressive Association contributed this float for Akron's 1925 Centennial parade. *Akron–Summit County Public Library.*

Hellenic Educational Progressive Association (AHEPA), which was formed in Georgia in response to discrimination Greek immigrants faced from the Ku Klux Klan. Akron's chapter, AHEPA #63, was active from its very beginnings, organizing relief drives for Greek refugees during and following both world wars. In just a few months during 1943, the association raised almost $350,000 from Akron's Greek population of six hundred. It also distributed *The Broadcaster*, a news-from-home newsletter sent to local Greek boys in the service. It was such a success that other AHEPA chapters around the country followed suit. In more recent years, the group's efforts have included the building of an apartment complex in Tallmadge that serves low-income seniors and people with disabilities.

Another early group was the Greek American Progressive Association, Damon and Pythias Lodge 17, which hosted the group's national convention here in 1935. Like the Italians, some clubs were formed by immigrants from particular regions of Greece. Immigrants from the island of Icaria joined the Chembithes chapter of the Pan Icarian Brotherhood, and those from the region of Arcadia found fellowship with the Niketaras Chapter #22 of the Pan-Arcadian Federation. The Pancretan Association of Akron was founded in 1931 by immigrants from the island of Crete.

Since the earliest days, women have been an active force behind many of these groups, serving on auxiliaries and organizing their own fundraisers. As early as 1923, the Greek Women's Club of the International Institute was meeting at the YWCA to sew for the Near East Relief Fund. Ladies who lived in East Akron belonged to the East Akron Greek Women's Club, which met at the East Akron Community House. One of the most active women's groups today is Annunciation Akron Philoptochos, or "Melissa," a ministry since 1927 of Annunciation Greek Orthodox Church. These hardworking ladies organize fundraisers throughout the year to benefit not only the church but also the community, with a special focus on veterans and the homeless.

RESTAURANTS AND FOOD BUSINESSES

No Greek festival, holiday or family gathering is complete without tables groaning with dishes from the homeland. Greeks love to cook and are proud to share their unique foods and culinary traditions. Nonagenarian Sarah Chibis says that "no Greek hostess would be caught dead without a homemade pastry to serve neighbors and friends who might drop by. We share our joy of cooking and eating, and our secret ingredient to a delicious meal is love." Since the turn of the twentieth century, Akron's Greeks have been sharing their family food traditions and making their mark on Akron's food and restaurant history.

In addition to the early fruit stands and coffeehouses, confectioneries and groceries were businesses typically owned by Greeks. Once his fruit stores became a success, Nick Laskaris expanded his offerings to candy and his handmade cigarette brand, Egyptian Crown. In July 1895, the *Akron Daily Democrat* reported that every fruit stand in the city was closed so Akron Greeks could attend a picnic organized by Laskaris. Nick "the Ice Cream Man" Chamberlain (Tsamperlas) and his brother, Andrew, were also early downtown food entrepreneurs, establishing an ice cream parlor in 1913 at Main and Exchange Streets. They later manufactured ice cream and, in 1907, opened one of Akron's first moving picture theaters, the Crystal Maze.

Western Fruit and Candy was started in 1916 by Trifon "Tom" Zaharopoulos, a native of Bytina, Greece. In the 1950s, it expanded to a wholesale operation; however, the retail store remained on East Market Street. It was owned continuously by folks of Greek descent until closing in 2020. In 1919, Pearl Coffee Company celebrated one hundred years of business as roasters and suppliers of fine coffee. It is still operated by members

This 1969 photo of Nicholas Economou, a founder of Pearl Coffee, was taken at the company's fiftieth-anniversary celebration. *Pearl Coffee Company*.

of the Economou family, descendants of the four brothers who founded it. A beloved downtown fixture was Harry Stelatos, the "Pushcart Man," who sold popcorn and nuts from a cart until he retired in 1957. Although later on the scene, Temo's Candy, established in 1947 by Christ and Areti Temo, supplied its loyal customers with handmade chocolates until 2020. On the east side of town, Akron's Greeks patronized Chibis Grocery on Thornton Street, owned for fifty years by Gus Chibis until he retired in 1961.

As coffeehouses and confectioneries became more successful, some evolved into restaurants and taverns, marking the beginning of a rich legacy of Greek-owned restaurants in Akron. One of the earliest was unnamed until owner John Pastis advertised a naming contest for his East Market Street eatery, which opened in 1919. An *Akron Beacon Journal* reader won ten dollars for suggesting the winning name, the Regal Restaurant. John and other members of the Pastis family were known over the years as restaurant and wholesale food business owners. Mike Pastis founded Summit Foods, which ran multiple fast-food establishments in the area. He also owned the Egg Castle restaurants.

Many beloved Akron restaurants were started by Greek immigrants, and some are still Greek-owned. When Akronites hear the name Parasson, most of us think of good, reasonably priced Italian fare. However, when George Paraskevopoulos opened his first restaurant on North Howard Street, he didn't serve pasta or pizza. The Parasson's we know today was started in 1960 by Tony, George's son, who made and sold pizza for his mother Sylvia's tavern in Barberton. The Anthe brothers, Charles and Nick, were known for their long-established fine-dining restaurants. Charles and his wife, Pauline, ran Anthe's Paradise in the 1950s, later opening Anthe's on Manchester Road. Nick's first place was located on Tallmadge Avenue until moving to a building on North Main. Everyone remembers his iconic eyeglass logo, which adorned matches, napkins and cocktail glasses. In 1957, John Bahas opened his Waterloo Restaurant in a former drive-up in South Akron. Over more than sixty years, it grew to be one of Akron's most popular family restaurants and catering venues. The Girves family still owns one of the area's best-loved steakhouses, the

Located at 52 East Market Street, Kimon and Gus Papageorge's Barbecue-Matic restaurant featured a special charcoal rotisserie grill that was visible and vented to the street. *Akron–Summit County Public Library.*

Brown Derby. Gus Girves's first restaurant located on East Market Street was open around the clock and a favorite of Akron's rubber workers, who could easily pop in after their shifts. He would go on to open multiple Brown Derby restaurants in Akron, as well as in other states. They are now owned and operated by his son Parris and grandson Parry. In 2014, Gus' Chalet, located for forty years on East Tallmadge Avenue, closed its doors. A favorite gathering spot for local politicians, it was owned by Gus Kanarios, who got his start working for the Anthe brothers. Mark Figetakis is known for his chain of Mark restaurants that expanded beyond Akron to Pennsylvania, Indiana and Florida. The restaurant business was in the blood of James Goumas, who owned downtown's Western Drive-In until it closed in 1971. In 1961, Robert Kalos opened the Bunny Drive-In on Copley Road. Named after his wife, Delores "Bunny" Kalos, the restaurant was known for its buckets of crispy fried chicken. Their son, Charles, took over in 1988, added his award-winning ribs and renamed it Charlie's Ribs and Chicken. In the 1970s and '80s, a new generation of Greek-owned bars and restaurants opened in town, including Nicky's, Asteria, Taki's Greek Tavern, Kalymnos Greek Tavern and Zorba's. Some even offered Greek dancing and plate breaking. Greek pastries and other delicacies could be bought in the 1970s and 1980s at Quaker Square's Sweet Greek, owned by Sarah Chibis and her daughters.

A 1972 *Akron Beacon Journal* article about Annunciation Church quotes a parishioner who described what it means to be Greek. *Philotimo* is the word he used. Loosely translated, it means "self-respect, integrity and pride." For Greeks, it extends to pride in one's community and always doing the right thing. Akron's Greek American community continues to embrace these tenets, and we can thank them for what they have brought to our history and culture.

Kalee Orexee!

Mary (Nurches) Ciesa

According to Mary, every good Greek family knows how to prepare this traditional rice soup. It is her family's go-to remedy for treating the common cold and a Sunday favorite. Mary's recipe was handed down by her Greek and Albanian ancestors. Her Albanian American mother, Artemis (Matzules), and Greek American father, Orpheus Nurches, taught their children the trick to keep the broth from curdling. A nurse practitioner, Mary writes and publishes children's books, including *Dina Prima the Ballerina*, later adapted for ballet and performed by the Wayne Center for the Arts Ballet Company.

Avgolemono Soup

1 chicken
2 quarts water (or 6 cups prepared chicken broth)
Salt
1 large onion, chopped
1 cup uncooked white rice
3 eggs, separated
Juice of 1 lemon, or more

To make chicken broth: In a large pot, cover chicken with 2 quarts of water or broth. Add salt and bring to a boil. Add chopped onion. Cover, lower heat and let simmer for 1 hour. Skim off any froth that floats to the top. Strain broth and set cooked chicken aside. Bring strained broth to a rolling boil and add rice. Stir so that rice does not stick to the pan. Cover with a heavy lid. When rice is cooked (about 15 minutes), lower the heat and let it simmer.

Meanwhile, in a large mixing bowl, beat 3 egg whites until stiff. Fold in yolks, if desired. Add the lemon juice slowly, beating well. (More lemons make it more lemony.) Add broth to the egg mixture a little at a time until most of the broth is used. Pour this mixture back into the pot, stirring well so it will not curdle. Add shredded or chopped pieces of chicken, if desired.

Ortha (Mollis) Cherpas

Ortha Mollis was born in 1925 in McKeesport, Pennsylvania, and came to Akron as a girl with her Greek immigrant parents, James and Mary (Douras) Mollis. She graduated from Central Hower High School, where she was a majorette and the school's 1941 May Queen. She met her future husband, Chris Cherpas, when both worked at the Sanitary Confectionery, a candy store on North Firestone Boulevard owned by Steve Vasiliou, a native of Tinos, Greece. Chris was fifteen and she was fourteen when they met. They were married in 1946 and raised three children: Maria, Chris and Patricia. While Chris practiced law with his firm, Cherpas, Manos and Syracopoulos, Ortha volunteered for numerous organizations, including Weathervane Playhouse and Annunciation Greek Orthodox Church, where she helped to oversee the icon painting of the sanctuary. She was an outstanding golfer, accomplished photographer and beloved for the Greek delicacies and baked goods she made for her family and friends. Her niece Maria-Elena Mollis recalled the pharmacist's desk in Ortha's basement kitchen that was filled with hundreds of cookie cutters, some custom-made by Ortha. *Contributed by Ortha's husband, Chris Cherpas.*

Moussaka

¼ cup olive oil
1 tablespoon butter
1 cup finely chopped onion
½ cup finely chopped parsley
2 cloves garlic, minced
1 pound ground beef
1 cinnamon stick
½ teaspoon salt
¼ teaspoon pepper
¾ cup red wine
3 tablespoons tomato paste
2 eggs, lightly beaten
2 medium eggplants, cut into ½-inch slices
¼ cup olive oil
Salt and pepper
¼ cup fine bread crumbs

Bechamel Sauce

½ cup butter
½ cup flour
2 cups warm milk
½ teaspoon salt
3 eggs, beaten
1 cup grated Parmesan cheese
Dash nutmeg

Heat oil and butter in large skillet. Sauté onion until golden. Add parsley, garlic, beef, cinnamon stick, salt and pepper. Cook until meat is lightly browned. Stir wine and tomato paste together and blend into meat mixture. Add ½ cup water and simmer for 20 minutes, or until most of liquid has been absorbed. Allow to cool.

Blend eggs into cooled meat mixture and set aside. Brush each side of eggplant with oil and sprinkle with salt and pepper. Broil until golden brown, turning once.

Make bechamel: In a medium saucepan, melt butter over low heat. Blend in flour until smooth. Gradually blend in milk. Add salt. Cook, stirring constantly until thickened and smooth. Remove from heat. Gradually beat eggs into sauce. Add cheese and nutmeg. Set aside.

Sprinkle bread crumbs evenly over bottom of a buttered 9x9 baking pan. Arrange one-third of eggplant slices in pan. Cover with half of meat mixture. Add another layer of eggplant and meat mixture and top with remaining eggplant. Pour bechamel sauce over all. Bake uncovered at 350 degrees for 1 hour or until top is golden.

Despina (Xenakis) Pastis

Katina Radwanski's great-grandfather Gust Pastis emigrated from Icaria, Greece, to New York City in 1900. He soon made his way to Akron and, over the next few years, made trips back to Greece, returning with his wife, Calliope, and their children, including Katina's grandfather James (Demetrious), who came in 1910. Soon after arriving, James found work as a chef, and by the early 1920s he was working alongside his brothers at their family-owned Sanitary Kitchen restaurant on South Main Street and the Savoy on East Market. He later worked at the Brown Derby as a chef. James and his wife, Despina, had four children, including Katina's father, Gus. Katina's cousin Christina, who lives in Greece, provided Despina's recipe for soufiko, a traditional Icarian dish. Katina remembers fondly the sounds and smells of her grandparents' cooking—Despina in the upstairs kitchen and James in the basement kitchen. *Contributed by Despina's granddaughter Katina (Pastis) Radwanski.*

Soufiko

2 to 2½ pounds zucchini
1 medium eggplant
2 green peppers
2 to 3 medium onions
2 large or 3 medium potatoes
3 cloves garlic, minced
2 to 3 tablespoons olive oil
¼ cup chopped parsley
Salt and pepper

Slice zucchini, eggplant, peppers, onion and potatoes into ¼-inch to ½-inch slices. Salt and let them sit at room temperature to remove excess water.

Sauté garlic in olive oil. Add parsley, salt and pepper. Add vegetables and fry a bit, adding potato toward the end. Pour into casserole or Dutch oven.

Cover and bake at 350 degrees until vegetables are tender and excess water has evaporated.

Sophia (Tzelissis) Vernis

Sophia came to Akron in 1954 from Athens, Greece, as a new bride with her husband, Thomas (Themistocles), a native of Rethymnon, Crete, who had arrived in the United States in 1914. Thomas lived in various places before putting down roots in Akron. In the early 1940s, he opened Vernis Jewelry, located at 5 West Market Street. By then an established and respected businessman, his only remaining task was to find a Greek wife, so back to Greece he traveled. He went to Sophia's family's house in Athens because he was told the family had a beautiful bridal prospect, Sophia's older sister Katina. Katina wasn't home, and her sister Sophia answered the door.

The rest is history. Thomas and Sophia married in Greece and returned to Akron, where they raised their children, Myron and Chryse, and were members of Annunciation Greek Orthodox Church. Actively involved in Melissa Philoptochos, Sophia lent her cooking skills to many church events, including the annual Greek Festival, where her pastitsio is one of the most popular items on the menu. Her daughter-in-law, Kim, has overseen the making of Sophia's recipe for more than twenty years. *Submitted by Sophia's daughter-in-law, Kim (Cabot) Vernis.*

Pastitsio

Noodle Layer
2 pounds ziti or penne noodles
½ stick butter
6 eggs, beaten
1 cup Romano cheese

Meat Sauce
4 pounds ground chuck
1 large onion, chopped
2 cloves garlic, minced
1 (28-ounce) can crushed tomatoes
⅛ cup chopped parsley
2 to 3 teaspoons cinnamon
½ teaspoon nutmeg
Salt and pepper

Crema
2½ sticks butter
7 tablespoons corn flour
6 cups milk, heated
1 cup milk mixed with 3 tablespoons cornstarch
6 eggs, beaten
3 cups Romano cheese

Boil noodles. Drain and toss with butter. Let cool and toss with eggs and cheese. Reserve a few handfuls for topping later. Spread in a greased 11 x 18 pan sprinkled with corn flour.

Brown meat with onion and garlic. Add tomatoes, parsley, spices and salt and pepper to taste. Spread over noodle layer, completely covering noodles. Lightly spread reserved noodles over the meat layer. This helps to hold up the crema.

Melt butter. Add corn flour and stir to blend. Slowly add warm milk, stirring constantly. Add the milk and cornstarch mixture and stir until very thick. Remove from heat and trickle in eggs, stirring quickly. Stir in cheese. Pour over the meat sauce layer, leaving at least ¼-inch clearance at the top of the pan.

Bake at 400 degrees for ½ hour. Reduce heat to 350 degrees and bake for an additional ½ hour, until the top is slightly browned.

Phaidra (Zervos) Retikas

Phaidra was born in Akron in 1927 to Panagiota and Andonius Zervos, Akron's first Greek doctor. She grew up in a traditional Greek home where the customs of their homeland were honored and observed. Education was paramount, and Phaidra went on to pursue a master's degree in English from Columbia University. At the encouragement of a relative, Demetrios Retikas came to Akron in 1953 from Greece to meet Phaidra, who was instantly smitten with the handsome doctor. Three months later they were married. Daughter Aphroditi "Diti" was born nine months later, followed by their son, Anthony. Phaidra was an accomplished Greek cook and gracious hostess. After her mother died in 2018, Diti found pages of meticulous notes Phaidra kept for every event she hosted, whether a bridge party, cookout or holiday. Each entry included Phaidra's menu, names of guests, what worked, what didn't and notes for improving recipes. Between entertaining, raising a family and teaching at the University of Akron and Litchfield Junior High, Phaidra found time to volunteer for numerous community organizations. She chaired Annunciation Greek Orthodox Church's annual festival during its earliest years and fought to move the one-room Greek bazaar from Main Street to the church. She reigned for twenty-five years as the "Queen of Souzoukakia," organizing and supervising the making of 3,500 meatballs for the annual festival. Diti received so many requests for the recipe, she whittled it down for home cooks. *Submitted by Phaidra's daughter, Aphroditi "Diti" (Retikas) Ciraldo.*

Souzoukakia

Meatballs
1 pound ground beef
2 eggs
1 teaspoon oregano
1 teaspoon salt
1 teaspoon pepper
1 cup dry bread crumbs, moistened with water
1 grated onion

Sauce
2 tablespoons tomato paste diluted in 3 cups of water
½ cup red wine
1 teaspoon salt
½ teaspoon cinnamon
½ teaspoon sugar
½ teaspoon minced garlic
½ teaspoon cumin

Mix all meatball ingredients. Roll into ovals, place on baking sheet and bake at 350 degrees for about 20 minutes.

Combine sauce ingredients in a saucepan and bring to a boil. Reduce heat to medium and simmer for 20 minutes. Add meatballs and simmer for an additional 30 minutes.

Note: Because Phaidra never wrote down measurements for seasonings, the amounts listed here are suggestions. According to Diti, she guesstimates and "so should you—that's what makes cooking fun!"

Polly Paffilas

Described by a colleague as one of the grande dames of journalism, Polly was a colorful fixture at the *Akron Beacon Journal*, where she was an award-winning reporter, food writer, women's page editor and "About Town" columnist. She clipped and indexed every recipe that appeared in the paper and kept them in tidy boxes until donating them to the Akron–Summit County Public Library, where they may now be researched via an online database. When she died in 2005, her nephew Steven described her as "proud to be Greek, caring, giving, strong-willed, hard-working, and meticulous." Spanakopita was one of her specialties, always served during the holidays, dinner parties and family get-togethers—long before spanakopita became a mainstay at wedding receptions and cocktail parties, according to Steven. Polly taught him to make it when he was in college, stressing that you had to work fast with the phyllo and never skimp on the butter. *Submitted by Polly's nephew Steven Paffilas.*

Spanakopita

2 pounds fresh spinach or 2 (10-ounce) packages of frozen, chopped spinach
1 medium onion, finely chopped
1 pound plus 4 tablespoons butter
1 cup medium bechamel sauce (made with butter)
8 eggs, well beaten
2 cups feta cheese, finely crumbled
1 tablespoon sugar
Dash of nutmeg
Salt and pepper to taste
1 package frozen phyllo dough

If using fresh spinach, wash thoroughly. Discard stems, dry and chop into coarse pieces. If using frozen, thaw and squeeze out excess water.

Sauté onion in 4 tablespoons of butter until soft. Add spinach and cook a few minutes more. Set aside to cool.

Combine bechamel sauce, eggs, feta, sugar, nutmeg, salt and pepper. Feta is salty, so beware of adding too much salt. Add spinach.

Butter an 11x15 pan. Melt remaining butter. Place two sheets of phyllo in pan. Brush with melted butter. Repeat until you have used 12 sheets. Spread spinach mixture on top. Top with 12 more sheets of phyllo, repeating the process used for the bottom layer. Brush top with butter.

Bake at 350 degrees for 50 to 60 minutes, or until crust is golden brown, puffed up and pulled away from the sides. Cut into 2-inch squares.

Maria (Cherpas) Eliason

Maria grew up in Akron, the daughter of Chris and Ortha Cherpas. A graduate with the first class at Firestone High School, she moved to Chicago in 1972, becoming a computer programmer in 1982. After moving back to Ohio in 1997, she worked as a programmer for Progressive Insurance, retiring in 2016. Her mother gave this recipe to her when she was in the seventh grade. Though it is originally from a Greek church cookbook, Maria has perfected it over the years—her version makes "long elegant cookies" rather than the traditional thicker ones. According to Maria, this recipe "makes a lot of dough—enough for the village."

Koulouria

1 tablespoon vanilla
½ cup milk
7 large eggs, room temperature
1 cup unsalted butter, room temperature
2 cups sugar
9½ cups flour
2 tablespoons baking powder
1 teaspoon salt
1 egg yolk
Sesame seeds

Mix vanilla into milk. Beat eggs lightly and set aside. Cream butter, gradually adding sugar until mixed thoroughly. Add eggs to butter and sugar mixture. Mix thoroughly.

Sift flour, baking powder and salt together. Add to wet mixture, alternating with milk. Knead dough on lightly floured surface. Divide dough and shape into two log-like rolls. Refrigerate before shaping. Tightly wrapped dough may be kept in the refrigerator for a few days.

To shape the koulouria: Roll out a rope twice as long as the final koulouria. Make a loop in the middle of the rope. Rest a butter knife on the top of the loop to keep it from shifting while braiding. Braid by moving one "leg" to the opposite side, 5 to 6 times. Cut off loose end. Keep unused dough chilled to make this process easier.

Place on cookie sheet (may be lined with parchment) and brush each with egg yolk mixed with I tablespoon of water. Sprinkle with sesame seeds. Bake on rack in upper third of oven at 350 degrees for 15 to 20 minutes.

Sarah Chibis

Gus Chibis was barely a teenager in 1910 when he left his village on the Greek island of Icaria to join his cousins in Warren. Within a few years, Argiro (Sylvia) Fountouli, also from Icaria, was sent by her family to marry Gus, who by then had moved to Akron. Although their 1922 marriage was arranged, they were blessed with seven children and remained happily married until Gus died in 1969. Gus, who was known in the Greek community for his poetry and extemporaneous recitations, owned the Square Deal grocery store on East Thornton Street for fifty years. Daughter Sarah, born in 1923, graduated from the old South High School and later worked at Goodyear Aircraft, where she helped to construct dirigibles. In 1976, she and her daughters, Aphrodite "Rita" Kasapis and Argiro "Paula" Kasapis, put their baking skills together and opened the Sweet Greek at the new Quaker Square. For several years, they sold pastries and other Greek specialties, including melomakarona, which is Sarah's favorite pastry. According to Sarah, it's not overly sweet and goes well with coffee but is also festive enough for a holiday. Also known as finikia or phoenikia, they are thought to have been introduced to Greece by the Phoenicians as early as 300 BC. Melomakarona are often served during Christmas, but because they don't contain dairy or eggs, they are also a favorite Lenten treat. Sarah fondly remembers how quickly her mother shaped them using a specially carved wooden spoon.

Melomakarona

Syrup
2 cups sugar
I cup water
Dash of lemon juice
I cinnamon stick

Cookies
1 cup sugar
1 ¼ cups orange juice
2 cups plus 3 tablespoons oil (canola, vegetable or olive)
4 teaspoons baking powder
½ teaspoon baking soda
2 teaspoons cinnamon (plus more for topping)
½ teaspoon nutmeg
8 cups (or less) flour
½ cup chopped walnuts for topping

Place sugar, water, lemon juice and cinnamon stick in a saucepan and bring to a boil. Reduce heat and simmer for 30 minutes. Turn off heat and leave on burner.

In a large bowl, whisk together sugar, orange juice, oil, baking powder, baking soda, cinnamon and nutmeg. Add flour slowly, mixing with hands until batter stiffens. Dough will feel oily and a little spongy. Break off small pieces of dough and shape into ovals. Place on lightly greased baking sheet. Use a fork to imprint a design on the top of each cookie, pressing fork horizontally from sides to top. Bake at 300 degrees for about 30 minutes. Allow to cool.

Reheat syrup to simmer. Drop cookies into syrup, top side down, allowing them to soak long enough to absorb a little syrup. Lift out with a slotted spoon and arrange on a platter. Top immediately with walnuts and sprinkle with cinnamon. Allow to cool. Keep in airtight container in refrigerator for up to two weeks or in the freezer for several months.

Mary (Markakis) Detorakis and Koula (Migadakis) Detorakis

The Detorakis family came to Akron from the city of Heraklion, Crete. John Michael Detorakis came to Akron by special invitation from his uncle and aunt George and Eugenia Kaniadakis. After becoming an American citizen, he returned to Crete in 1957 and married Mary Markakis. The couple settled in Akron, where John worked for Harwick Chemical and later as an electronic technician for Firestone Tire and Rubber. In 1965, John's brother Evangelos Michael Detorakis came to Akron, returning to Crete and marrying Koula Migadakis. Angelo worked for the Goodyear

Tire and Rubber Company and later owned and operated Western Fruit Basket. Koula and Evangelos "Angelo" prepared authentic Greek food, pastries and fruit baskets for over twenty years. Both families have been active members of the Cretan Association of Akron and the Pancretan Association of America. Important to the Detorakis families is preserving recipes and sharing them through baking workshops with the newest generation of the family. Baklava is a favorite at weddings, baptisms, holidays and especially Christmas. John and Mary's daughter Toula has taught many friends and family members how to make this baklava, a recipe from her mother, Mary, and Aunt/Thea Koula. When one of her students shared this Greek favorite, a guest exclaimed, "Where did you learn to make this baklava? I know only one person who makes it this way!" Sure enough, she learned from Toula. *Submitted by Mary's daughter and Koula's niece Toula (Detorakis) Elefter.*

Baklava

Syrup
3 cups sugar
2 cups water
2 tablespoons honey
1 teaspoon fresh lemon juice
1 cinnamon stick
5 whole cloves

Baklava
1 cup sugar
6 cups finely chopped walnuts (about 2 pounds)
1 teaspoon cinnamon
½ teaspoon cloves
1 ½ pounds phyllo dough
1 pound butter, melted and clarified

Mix sugar and water in a saucepan. Bring to boil and cook over medium heat for 15 to 20 minutes. Add honey, lemon juice, cinnamon stick and cloves. Simmer for an additional 5 to 8 minutes. Set aside and cool. Syrup will thicken slightly as it cools. Strain to remove cinnamon and cloves. Set aside and cool to room temperature.

Combine sugar, walnuts and spices and set aside. Butter an 11x17 baking pan. Layer 12 sheets of phyllo in pan, buttering each layer. Sprinkle half of the walnut mixture on the 12th sheet. Layer 2 more sheets over the walnuts. Sprinkle the remaining walnut mixture on top. Add 12 more sheets, buttering each layer. Refrigerate for 15 minutes and then score into diamonds or triangles.

   Bake at 350 degrees for 40 to 45 minutes or until golden brown on the top and bottom. Check the bottom by lifting with a spatula. Remove from oven and cut along score marks. Drizzle the syrup carefully over hot baklava. Start with the perimeter of the pan followed by the scored/cut sections and, finally, the top of each piece. Let baklava sit overnight to allow syrup to absorb.

Noula (Poleondakis) Kountis

Noula's father, George Poleondakis, left Crete in 1912 to come to America. Just sixteen years old, he settled first in Massachusetts, later working in the coal mines of West Virginia, finally settling in Akron. In 1952, he returned to Crete and married Anthoula Rodoussakis. When George died in 1973, Anthoula was left with raising their children—Noula, Tony and John—working as a seamstress to support and educate them. She was beloved for her infectious smile, love of life and her cooking, the glue that brought her family and friends together. Kalitsounia is a traditional Cretan sweet, and this version is from Chania. Tsikoudia, a grape-based liquor made in Crete, is also used as a remedy for multiple ailments. Noula is an active member of Akron's Pancretan Association, as were her parents. In 2013, she helped to coordinate the national convention held in Akron.

Haniotika Kalitsounia

Filling
2 pounds ricotta cheese
12 ounces dry cottage cheese
1 (8-ounce) package cream cheese
1 cup sugar
2 eggs
1 to 2 teaspoons crushed fresh mint leaves

Dough

1 cup water
1 cup butter-flavored vegetable shortening
¼ cup vegetable oil
1 egg
Salt
5½ cups flour, plus more if needed
*¼ cup Tsikoudia (if not available, substitute 1 teaspoon lemon juice mixed with 2
teaspoons baking powder)*
Vegetable oil for frying
Sugar and cinnamon for topping

In a large bowl, mix filling ingredients and set aside.

Mix all dough ingredients, adding more flour if necessary to make a firm dough. Knead well. Roll dough to make a thin sheet. A pasta maker works well for this. Start at setting 1, finishing with setting 5. Using a teacup saucer or round plastic lid, cut circle shapes into the dough, approximately 5 to 6 inches in diameter. Fill each with 1 tablespoon of filling. Fold dough over to form a half-circle and seal edges with a fork.

Heat 1 inch of vegetable oil in a large frying pan. Fry until golden, turning once. Remove and drain on paper towels. While still warm, sprinkle with sugar and cinnamon. Best when served warm.

Chryse (Vernis) Brown

Chryse was born in 1957 in Rethymnon on the Greek island of Crete. When doctors told her parents that her cerebral palsy was serious and that there was little they could do for her, Chryse's parents, Thomas and Sophia Vernis, moved her and her brother Myron to Akron, where Thomas had lived for a few years before returning to Greece. Thomas and Sophia, along with what was then United Cerebral Palsy of Akron, worked to see that she had every advantage and service available to her. As Chryse was strong-willed and positive, nothing stood in her way. She graduated from North High School and was hired in 1979 by the Akron–Summit County Public Library, where she worked in the Technical Services department for thirty-four years. It was there that she met her husband, David Brown. Chryse enjoys her golden retrievers, cooking, gardening and painting and is an active volunteer for Akron Children's Hospital, Annunciation Greek Orthodox Church Sunday School and the Northampton–Cuyahoga Falls Historical Society. Chryse inherited her cooking skills and Greek recipes from her mother, Sophia. Tsoureki, a traditional Easter bread, is one of her family's most treasured family recipes. It was handed down by her grandmother Amalia (Droudakis) Tzelissis.

Tsoureki

2 cups water
3 to 4 cinnamon sticks
1 handful whole cloves
Dried rind of 1 orange
1 pound butter
1 quart whole milk
2 to 3 packets active dry yeast
2½ pounds plus 1 tablespoon sugar for dissolving yeast
1 teaspoon mahlepi (optional: ground pits of a Persian cherry tree available online or at Greek specialty stores)
1 teaspoon masticha (liqueur of the mastic tree available online or at Greek specialty stores)
12 eggs, plus 1 or 2 more for brushing on top of shaped loaves
10 pounds flour

Boil 2 cups of water. Add cinnamon sticks, cloves and orange rind. Let steep for at least 30 minutes or overnight. If steeped overnight, warm before using.

In medium saucepan, melt butter with ½ of milk. Once butter has melted, remove from heat and add remaining milk.

In a metal bowl, dissolve yeast in 1½ cups of the warm spice water. Add 1 tablespoon sugar, mahlepi and masticha. Set aside to activate yeast.

In large bowl, mix remaining sugar and 12 eggs until well beaten. Add butter and milk mixture. Mix well. Add a few cups of flour and then the yeast mixture. Add remaining flour until dough is thick and just a bit sticky. If needed, more flour may be added prior to shaping. Allow to rise 4 to 6 hours or, preferably, overnight.

Punch down and let rest for 1 hour. Divide dough into roughly 1-pound balls and shape as desired. Place on parchment-lined baking sheet. Let rise 1 to 2 hours. Brush gently with beaten eggs.

Bake in 350-degree oven for 20 to 30 minutes or until golden brown. Remove from baking sheets and cool. Makes 12–14 loaves.

HUNGARIAN

When Jennifer Jacobs collects honey and eggs on her Copley Township farm, she honors the work of her grandparents and great-grandparents who began farming the land more than one hundred years ago. In 1919, Jennifer's Hungarian immigrant great-grandparents Frank and Agnes Jacobs bought the farmstead, where they lived as they did in the old country, growing crops to sell, as well as what they needed for themselves. Frank and Agnes were among many Hungarian immigrant truck farmers who bought farms and settled in Copley Township. Jennifer's family is one of the thousands of Hungarians who made Akron and Summit County home. Many came to the United States following the 1848 revolution; however, the earliest to arrive in Summit County came just before the turn of the twentieth century. A 1911 *Akron Beacon Journal* article about Hungarians in Akron estimated that more than six thousand Hungarians were living here at that time. After World War I and the breakup of the Austro-Hungarian Empire, that number increased dramatically as Hungarians fled their native lands, many flocking to northeastern Ohio. Akron's booming rubber industry drew a great number of these immigrants, especially young men, many of whom intended to stay and work here temporarily until returning home with their earnings. Although some returned to Hungary, the majority stayed here and became citizens. Not all settled in Akron, though. Barberton was a popular destination for eastern European immigrants, including Hungarians. The Displaced Persons Act of 1948 and the Hungarian

Revolution of 1956 brought another wave; many came to join family or were offered sponsorship by one of the churches or benevolent societies that helped them to leave Hungary.

WHERE THEY LIVED

Most of the early immigrants settled in and around Goosetown, where they established social clubs, businesses and churches. Although the majority were employed as laborers in Akron's industries, some returned to their agricultural roots, moving outside the city to buy and operate small farms. Others settled in and around Barberton, taking jobs with that city's growing industries. Like the Germans, Akron's Hungarians had their own newspapers. *Het* (*Week*) and *Akroni Magyar Hirlap* (*Akron Hungarian Journal*) were weekly papers that reported community news, politics and advertisements.

CHURCH LIFE

Although many of Akron's earliest Hungarian immigrants were Jews, the majority of later immigrants were Protestant and Catholic. The Hungarian Reformed Church was the first to organize in 1914 with just 12 members. Within a year, the congregation grew to more than 250 and bought the former St. John's Lutheran building on Coburn Street. In 1933, a group of members split, forming the Independent Reformed Hungarian Church and moving to a building on West Thornton Street. In 1965, the congregation dedicated a new building on Copley Road to better serve its members, most of whom no longer lived in the old Goosetown neighborhood. The name was changed to Christ Reformed Church. Soon after the church's dedication, Bishop Tibor Domotor assumed the position of pastor. According to his wife, Elizabeth, one of his first goals was to reconnect Akron's divided Hungarian Reformed Churches, a task that some of his church members deemed impossible. Undeterred, he worked with both churches to heal old wounds. Within three years, the Copley church reconnected and merged with the Coburn Street church, then known as First Hungarian Church of God. After the Hungarian Revolution of 1956, the church sponsored more than 1,500 Hungarian

The Independent Hungarian Reformed Church, located at 419 West Thornton Street.
Akron Beacon Journal Collection, Summit Memory, Akron–Summit County Public Library.

refugees, offering them support and English classes. Christ Reformed Church still meets today at the Copley Road building, where services are conducted in English and Hungarian.

Hungarian Lutherans and Baptists formed congregations, too. First Hungarian Baptist was organized in 1920 and dedicated a new church at the corner of Voris and Washington Streets in 1924. By 1954, it had disbanded. First Hungarian Lutheran Church, located on Grant Street, operated from about 1928 to 1935. First Hungarian Pentecostal, later First Hungarian Assembly of God, served its congregation from the 1930s until about 1970.

If you were Roman Catholic, you likely attended Sacred Heart of Jesus Church, founded in 1915. In 1925, the congregation dedicated its new building at 734 Grant Street under the leadership of Father Pupinsky, who helped to organize the church. Sacred Heart was an anchor for Akron's Catholic Hungarian Americans, offering festivals, dinners and English language courses for new immigrants, including many who came after the 1956 revolution. Over the years, membership declined, and the church became a casualty of the reorganization and consolidation of churches by the Catholic Diocese of Cleveland. It closed in 2010.

Dancers at the Magyar Home on East Thornton Street during the annual Hungarian Grape Festival. 1940. *Akron Beacon Journal Collection, Summit Memory, Akron–Summit County Public Library.*

Members of the Magyar Home Singing Society at the club's ten-year jubilee in 1934. *Akron Beacon Journal Collection, Summit Memory, Akron–Summit County Public Library.*

Workers pose outside of the newly constructed Hungarian American Club on East Thornton Street, 1923. *Hungarian American Club.*

CLUBS AND ORGANIZATIONS

Akron's established Hungarian American immigrants were always ready to help the newly arrived. Benevolent and sick societies were formed to help them get settled, learn the new language and provide a place where their customs and foods could be shared and enjoyed. Whether you were interested in singing, athletics, politics, charity or war relief, there was a Hungarian club for everyone. The first was the Austrian-Hungarian Society, formed around 1895. Several clubs descended from the German-Hungarian Singing Society established in 1911. Various splits in that group resulted in the Austrian-Hungarian Military Sick Benefit Society and the German Hungarian Mutual Aid Society. By 1925, there were at least eighteen Hungarian clubs in Akron, including the Pioneer American Hungarian Club, Old Hungarian Settlers Society, Verhovy Aid Society, Hungarian Athletic Club, Rakoczi Society and the Hungarian Women's Club of the YWCA. The last remaining club is the Akron Hungarian American Club, located on East Waterloo Road. Its 1960s-era building includes an Art Deco–style back bar, a relic of the 1923 Akroni Magyar Hazhe building on East Thornton Street, which served as the hub of Hungarian social life until 1965, when it was torn down. Ground was broken that year for a new building, and by the summer of 1966, the club was proudly advertising its modern new home on East Waterloo. Most of today's club members are older; however, a group of young members has recently taken the helm, infusing new life into Akron's last Hungarian club.

A 1910 advertisement for the Royal Hungarian Gypsy Orchestra, a regular at the Black Whale Inn located at 125 South Main Street. *From the* Akron Beacon Journal.

RESTAURANTS AND FOOD BUSINESSES

If you weren't Hungarian but had a taste for old-country cuisine, Akron offered plenty of options outside of the members-only clubs. One of Akron's first Hungarian restaurants, simply called the Hungarian Restaurant, was located on Cherry Street. Hungarian music could be enjoyed along with your dinner at many local restaurants and taverns. In 1910, the Royal Hungarian Gypsy Orchestra performed at the Black Whale Inn at 125 South Main Street. The Famous Gypsy Love Orchestra headlined at Akron's Grand Opera House in 1917. In July 1919, Olmar's Music Hall and Restaurant at High and Mill Streets promised a "gypsy orchestra" and "a hot time in a cool place." Hall's "49" Lounge, which claimed to be Akron's "only continental restaurant and bar," featured a "gypsy grotto" and live Hungarian music. Johnny's Hideaway on South Arlington served daily specials of chicken paprikash, strudels and nut rolls—all beloved recipes from the mother of the owner, John Drotos. It closed in the early 1970s. Former police sergeant Joseph Merle opened his Hungarian restaurant, Josef's, in 1978. It was famous for its beef paprikash and Szekely goulash, as well as its friendly and comfortable ambiance. From 1961 until 1985, Mitchell Strauss served downtown workers at MiJo's House of Paprikash. According to a 1998 *Akron Beacon Journal* article published at the time of his death, he prided himself on serving delicious fare at a price his customers could afford. Traditional Hungarian fare is available today at Your Cabbage Connection, a carryout in Springfield Township.

In 1998, Akron Hungarian American Club president Thelma "Micki" Ladich wrote a piece for the group's seventy-fifth-anniversary commemorative book. She spoke of history, heritage and home as the guiding principles of the club. Those principles, held close by today's Akron's Hungarian American community, as well as a renewed enthusiasm by the next generations, will surely sustain and preserve their heritage for descendants and future generations of Akron's Hungarian Americans.

Jó étvágyat!

Margaret (Bajoczky) Kallas

According to grandson Miklos, this fusion of paprikash and spaghetti was created by his grandmother Margaret to please her Greek American husband, Pete, whom she married in 1933. Margaret was born in Olaszliszka, Hungary, in Zemplén County and arrived at Ellis Island on November 9, 1929, on the SS *Berengaria*. After following her father, Andy, to Akron, she took a job cleaning houses. According to Miklos, this is a versatile dish that can be adapted for sloppy joes, chili or chili-mac. It was made regularly in his home and always on hand for a quick meal. He especially enjoyed one of Margaret's versions that entailed frying leftover spaghetti noodles in lard, adding the spaghetti sauce and cooking it until it was crunchy, like bits of meatloaf. It was often served on fresh buttered bread from Cheda's Bakery. *Contributed by Margaret's grandson Miklos Peter Janosi.*

Hungarian Spaghetti Sauce

1 onion, minced
1 stalk celery, finely diced
1 large carrot, finely diced
1 to 3 cloves garlic, minced
1 to 3 tablespoons vegetable oil or lard
2 to 3 pounds ground beef
Salt and pepper
3 black peppercorns
1 (46-ounce) can tomato juice
Sweet Hungarian paprika

Sauté vegetables in lard or oil until the onions are glassy. Add the ground beef and salt and pepper and fry until brown. Add peppercorns and enough tomato juice to cover the meat, plus the width of a finger. Bring to a boil. Reduce heat to a slow boil and cook until the sauce thickens. When it is the consistency and flavor you like, add the paprika and salt and pepper to taste.

Note: Margaret used sweet paprika only, but Miklos adds hot paprika for some kick, as well as various spices such as parsley, oregano or ground caraway. He sometimes substitutes bloody Mary mix for tomato juice.

Elizabeth (Lazar) Toth

Elizabeth (Lazar) and John Toth came as young children to Barberton, the home of many Hungarian immigrants who settled in Summit County. John arrived in 1907 from the Tolna County region of Hungary, and Elizabeth, from Mezőkövesd, Hungary, came in 1913. They married in 1928 and had three children. John worked for Babcock & Wilcox in Barberton for fifty years, and Elizabeth was a homemaker. Their grandson John's interest in cooking and his family's history inspired him to keep the family's culinary traditions alive, even though his grandmother rarely used a cookbook or wrote her recipes down. The chicken paprikash recipe was passed down to him by Elizabeth. John is a proud member of the Hungarian Benefit Society in Barberton. *Contributed by Elizabeth's grandson John Toth.*

Chicken Paprikash

6 tablespoons butter
2 tablespoons olive oil
2 tablespoons paprika
2 large onions, chopped
8 chicken thighs, skins removed
2 chicken breasts, skins removed, cut into halves
2 cloves garlic, diced
1 teaspoon salt
1 teaspoon pepper
1 teaspoon crushed red pepper
1 tablespoon cornstarch

In a large pot, melt butter and olive oil over low heat. Add paprika and stir until combined, taking care not to burn the paprika. Add onions and sauté for about 2 minutes. Add chicken, garlic, salt, pepper and crushed red pepper. Mix until chicken is coated well. Cover pot and simmer on medium-low heat for 1 hour. Do not lift the lid while it is cooking. Whisk cornstarch in cold water. Stir into chicken and mix well. This helps to thicken the sauce.

Elizabeth (Guba) Domotor

Elizabeth arrived in Cleveland in 1957 following the Hungarian Revolution of 1956. She grew up in Szlep, Hungary, where her father was a researcher for a sugar factory. Upon her arrival in Cleveland, she discovered that her aunt who promised to host her had taken a trip to Hawaii. With nowhere to go, she found refuge in a Lutheran church. Soon she would meet Tibor Domotor, a young Hungarian freedom fighter from Budapest and assistant minister at her church. They married, had two children and moved to Akron in 1966, when her husband was tapped to lead Christ Reformed Church. A medical technologist, Elizabeth managed the blood laboratory at Akron's St. Thomas Hospital for many years. She is deeply involved with her church and today manages a small group home located on its grounds. Elizabeth recalled that her mother and grandmother were outstanding cooks and bakers; however, she learned little from them because she attended boarding school for much of her youth. She credits the ladies of her church for teaching her to cook. Szekely Gulyas is a favorite of her family, as well as residents at the group home. This recipe is included in *Hungarian Cookbook*, published by the Dorcas Guild of Christ Reformed Church.

Szekely Gulyas (Goulash)

3 tablespoons shortening, divided
1 onion, chopped
1 teaspoon paprika
2 cloves garlic, diced
1 teaspoon salt
½ teaspoon pepper
3 ounces tomato juice
2 pounds pork butt, diced
1 pound sauerkraut
1 head cabbage, sliced
1 tablespoon flour
1 cup sour cream

Melt 2 tablespoons of the shortening in a large skillet. Brown the onion. Add the paprika, garlic, salt, pepper, tomato juice and pork. Add ¼ cup of water. Cover and cook over low heat for 45 minutes.

In another skillet, melt the remaining tablespoon of shortening. Add the sauerkraut, cabbage and ¼ cup water. Cook until the cabbage is tender. Add flour and stir until mixed. Add this mixture to the meat along with sour cream. Mix thoroughly and serve.

Elizabeth (Grimm) Miller

Andrew Miller immigrated to Akron from Budapest in 1910. He was joined a year later by his wife, Elizabeth, and their three young son: Julius, Geza and Joseph. A daughter, Helen, and another son, Andrew, were born soon after. Born and raised in Budapest, Andrew and Elizabeth were ethnic Germans who brought their European culture and cooking customs with them. Elizabeth was a gifted cook and passed on her skills and recipes to her daughter, Helen. Helen's son, Robert Jeffries, inherited some of their recipes and cooking talents but was challenged the first time he attempted to make goulash. He was living in Phoenix at the time and did his best to re-create the recipe he remembered from watching his mother. It just wasn't the same, however. A phone call to his mother filled in some of the details, but it was still not quite right. After moving back to Ohio, he and his mother re-created step-by-step instructions for his grandmother's beloved recipe, which has been preserved in *Kitchen Keepsakes from the Miller Family*, a cookbook created for a family reunion. Although it is his grandmother's recipe, Robert is certain that it was enjoyed by multiple generations of his family. *Contributed by Elizabeth's grandson Robert Jeffries.*

Hungarian Goulash

1 ½ pounds beef round steak, bone-in, if available
½ cup extra virgin olive oil
3 tablespoons butter
30 ounces beef broth
1 (14½-ounce) can unseasoned, whole peeled tomatoes, cut into pieces
3 cups celery, chopped into medium-size pieces
1 large or 2 medium white or yellow onions, chopped into medium-size pieces
3 tablespoons Hungarian sweet paprika
1 clove garlic, minced
1 teaspoon salt

¾ teaspoon pepper
4 large potatoes, peeled and cubed
3 bay leaves

Trim fat from beef and cut into 1-inch cubes. Reserve bone. Place the olive oil and butter in a large skillet and brown beef over medium heat for 12 to 15 minutes, stirring occasionally for even browning. Do not overcook.

In a large stockpot or Dutch oven add the broth, tomatoes, celery, onion, paprika, garlic, salt, pepper and round steak bone. Add the beef and juices from the skillet. Bring to a medium boil. Reduce heat and cover. Simmer on stovetop for 1½ to 2 hours, or in oven at 350 degrees for 2½ to 3 hours until beef is tender, adding the potatoes and bay leaves during the last 45 minutes.

Note: Although some Hungarian cooks add thickeners such as flour, Robert's family does not. Peppers and other vegetables are not included in this recipe. As Robert's family might have said, "We are making goulash, not stew!"

Jennifer Jacobs

Jennifer grew up in a house that was built on the family farm by her mother, Mary Surowski. She spent lots of time with her Hungarian immigrant grandparents Frank and Vilma Jacobs, especially her grandmother Vilma and her uncle Frank, who did much of the farm work. In 1998, Jennifer took over the farm, where she now lives and farms much the way her Hungarian great-grandparents did. Jacobs Heritage Farm raises Mangalitsas (a breed of heritage Hungarian pigs), sheep, ducks, geese, quail and chickens, all for sale. Her honeybees are raised in a handcrafted Hungarian-style bee house, and the jars are decorated with Hungarian flowers. In Jennifer's words, "I put my heritage out there." Roast goose, a traditional Hungarian dish, is a family favorite. Jennifer hopes to raise awareness of roast goose as a delicious alternative to chicken or turkey.

Roast Goose

1 goose: When buying a whole duck or goose, allow about 1 to 1½ pounds of raw weight per person. Raw boneless meat yields about 3 servings per pound after cooking. Estimate 3 to 4 ounces per person for fully cooked products.

Salt and pepper
*Assorted vegetables: potatoes, carrots and onions work well, but use whatever you
like or have on hand*

Preheat oven to 400 degrees. Rinse goose thoroughly, pat dry and rub the outside and cavity of the goose with salt and a little pepper. After removing the obvious fat, prick the goose all over the skin with a skewer or other sharp tool, taking care not to pierce the meat. This gives the remaining fat an escape route during cooking. Save all extra fat. It's liquid gold and has many uses! Stuff goose with your favorite stuffing. This helps it cook more evenly and keeps the meat moist and tender.

Put the goose breast-side-down on a rack in a roasting pan. Add potatoes and other vegetables of your choice to the roasting pan. Place goose in oven, reduce heat to 375 degrees and cook 2 to 3 hours, depending on the size of the bird, usually about 20 minutes per pound. The skin should be crispy and dark brown, but not black. Goose is done when the legs move easily, juices run clear and a meat thermometer inserted into the thickest part of the thigh reads 180 degrees. Let rest 15 minutes before carving. Remove stuffing and serve with goose.

Emma (Jordan) Stracak

Emma was twenty-one when she emigrated in 1910 from Hungary with infant daughter, Emma, to join her husband, John, who arrived the year before. Emma and John settled in the heart of Goosetown, where they raised their six daughters. Their second daughter, Katherine, married Hungarian immigrant Steve Gulosh (Istvan Gulyas). Steve and Katherine's daughter, Katherine "Katy" Cole, was determined to find a way to reproduce her grandmother Emma's noodle recipe. In 2004, she reached out to the *Akron Beacon Journal*'s Recipe Roundup, a regular food section feature where readers shared and requested recipes. Two readers responded with their own family recipes for this rich noodle dish, one made with lard and the other with low-fat margarine. Katy's daughter Diane is pretty sure her mother opted for the lard version. According to Diane, "Great Gramma was feisty up into her older years and was still quite sharp playing Pepper, a variation of euchre. She was a lovely soul, and I don't think I ever heard her yell." *Contributed by Emma's great-granddaughter and Katy's daughter Diane (Cole) Barton.*

Farina Noodles

3 tablespoons lard
1 scant cup farina
2 teaspoons salt
2 cups boiling water
1 package medium noodles
½ cup butter, melted

Melt lard in cast-iron skillet. Add farina and fry until brown. Add salt and boiling water. Cover and let steam until thick and crumbly. Cook and drain noodles and add to farina. Pour melted butter over the mixture.

Nick Kozma

Nick Kozma's Hungarian parents, Nicholas and Elizabeth, first settled in New Jersey, later moving to Punxsutawney, Pennsylvania, and finally, to Wainwright, Ohio, where Nick was born in 1922. Soon after his birth, the family moved to Toledo, where they worked for the Heinz Company, picking tomatoes for five cents per bushel. When Nick was five, he and his father were in a car accident that killed his father. Soon after the accident, his mother moved her six children to Akron to be near family. Nick's oldest brother, John, quit school to take a job as a truck driver, and his sisters did house cleaning and babysitting to help out. Although they had little money, there was always food on the table. Nick went to Garfield High School, served in the Civilian Conservation Corps and the army and retired from Ohio Bell with forty-three years of service. He met his second wife, Mary Ann (Papp) Kurko, at Sacred Heart of Jesus Church. Until the church closed in 2010, Nick could be found there each month making kuglof to raise funds for the congregation. According to Mary Ann, the all-ladies baking group was initially suspicious of her husband's intention to join them, but he was soon one of the gang, helping to bake one hundred loaves of the sweet Hungarian bread each month. Mary Ann adapted this recipe from the original church recipe, which made sixteen loaves per batch. *Contributed by Nick's wife, Mary Ann (Papp) Kurko Kozma.*

Sacred Heart of Jesus Church Kuglof

2 cups plus 1 tablespoon sugar
¼ cup cinnamon
2 cups warm milk (divided, plus more for brushing loaves)
2 packages active dry yeast
4 egg yolks
½ pound margarine, softened
½ pound butter, softened
1 cup sour cream
1 teaspoon salt
10 to 12 cups flour
1 cup white raisins (optional)

Mix 1 cup of the sugar with cinnamon and set aside for sprinkling on the dough later. This addition to the bread is optional.

In a large bowl, mix 1 cup of warm milk, yeast and 1 tablespoon of sugar. Set aside. Mix 1 cup sugar, egg yolks, margarine, butter, sour cream and salt. Add to milk, yeast and sugar mixture. Mix well with an electric mixer. Add 10 cups of flour and the remaining cup of warm milk, adding additional flour as needed to make a soft and somewhat sticky dough. Mix for 15 to 20 minutes. If desired, fold in raisins.

Place dough in large, greased pan. Cover with plastic wrap and let rise until doubled in size, about 1 hour. Grease 4 or 5 loaf pans or 2 angel food cake pans. Divide dough into 4 or 5 pieces for loaf pans or 2 pieces for angel food pans. Place on a floured board, cover with cloth and let rise an additional 45 to 60 minutes. Roll out each piece of dough. If desired, sprinkle with cinnamon and sugar mixture. Twist gently, place in pans and let rise a third time until dough reaches the top of the pan. Brush with milk.

Bake at 350 degrees for 35 to 40 minutes, turning the pans halfway through the baking time. For a shiny glaze, you can brush the baked bread with a glaze made with milk into which a small amount of sugar has been dissolved.

Marjorie (Demeter) Houser

Sharon Moreland Myers remembers her small and feisty aunt Marjorie as "the best cook and baker ever." Marjorie was born in 1916 to Geza and Catherine Demeter, Hungarian immigrants who settled in Akron. She married Sharon's mother's brother, Roy Houser. Sharon's fondest memories are her aunt's after-church lunch spread that might include duck, chicken, leg of lamb, paprikash, Hungarian sausage and always a dessert. As Sharon recalled, "I remember her making strudel and stretching the filo dough on a floured, white sheet on the dining room table. She always ground her own nuts and cranberries. No shortcuts were taken!" Sharon is fairly certain that this recipe is from Aunt Marjorie's mother, Catherine. *Submitted by Marjorie's niece Sharon Moreland Myers.*

Criss Cross Cake

½ pound ground walnuts
1 ½ pounds butter, softened
2 cups flour
1 cup sugar
2 eggs
½ cup grape or other jelly

Mix the walnuts, butter, flour, sugar and eggs. Pat half of dough into a 9x12 pan. Spread jelly on top. With the remaining dough, make rolled pieces of dough and arrange on the cake in a crisscross design. Bake at 350 degrees for 40 to 45 minutes.

Charlotte Marky

In 1957, when Charlotte Marky was just fifteen years old, she made the difficult decision to leave her family and flee her home in Hungary for a life of freedom. After six harrowing days and several close encounters with Russian soldiers, she and her companions reached Yugoslavia, where, for more than a year, she lived in multiple internment camps. In vivid detail and with astounding recall, Charlotte tells the story of her childhood and escape from Hungary in *Journey to Freedom* (Tate Publishing, 2015), a chilling and at turns heartwarming account of her home and childhood during World War II, as well as life under Russian control following World War II. Charlotte's memories of life in rural Hungary and her new life in Akron include the foods of her family. Grandmother Katalin Csepregi was Charlotte's father's mother. Her chocolate torte with a light sponge cake and rich chocolate frosting has been a holiday and special occasion favorite of her family for four generations.

Grandmother Katalin's Chocolate Torte

Cake
9 eggs, separated
Pinch salt
9 tablespoons flour
1 teaspoon baking powder
9 tablespoons sugar
1 teaspoon vanilla extract
9 tablespoons grated semisweet baker's chocolate

Frosting
4 cups powdered sugar
3 squares unsweetened baker's chocolate, melted
1 teaspoon vanilla
2 sticks unsalted butter, softened
3 to 4 tablespoons milk or half-and-half

Beat egg whites with a pinch of salt until stiff peaks form. Set aside. In a separate bowl, mix together flour and baking powder.

With a mixer, cream the egg yolks with sugar and vanilla until lemon-colored. Add the grated chocolate. Add the flour and baking powder mixture. Gently fold the egg whites into the yolk batter. Do not overmix. It should be light and airy. Divide batter into 3 9-inch greased and floured cake pans. Bake at 375 degrees for 12 to 15 minutes. Watch carefully and do not overbake. If it springs back when touched with a fingertip, it is done. Cool a few minutes in the pan and invert onto a cooling rack.

To make the frosting, cream all ingredients together until light and fluffy. Frost each layer, stack layers and frost top and sides of the torte.

IRISH

The forgotten man in canal history is the common laborer, the largely unskilled worker who cleared trees, grubbed brush, muscled rocks, and, above all, dug the great ditches. His tools were…pick, shovel, scoop, ax, and wheelbarrow.

These words from historian George W. Knepper's essay in *Canal Fever: The Ohio & Erie Canal, from Waterway to Canalway* (Kent State University Press, 2009) describe the grueling work of the canal workers, the first Irishmen to arrive in Akron. When work began in July 1825 on the Ohio and Erie Canal, most of the laborers were Irishmen fresh from completing New York's Erie Canal. Their daily pay included room and board, thirty cents and a jigger of whiskey. Unmarried men lived together, and married men and their families lived in shanties in what was called Dublin located along the Little Cuyahoga River, just north of the city. The wives and daughters of these men also worked hard, supplementing the family income by working as cooks, seamstresses and laundresses. Some ladies were entrepreneurial, opening up boardinghouses and taverns. Life was tough, and diseases like smallpox, cholera and typhoid fever took many lives. It has been said that there was one dead Irishman for every three miles of canal.

WHERE THEY LIVED

The next wave of Irish to arrive in Akron were immigrants who fled the Potato Famine of the 1840s. Most were unskilled farmers who took whatever jobs they could find, working side by side with immigrants from other European countries. By the turn of the century, Akron was home to more than one thousand Irish-born residents, and although Akron's Dublin remained home to many Irish, an increasing number scattered to areas in the city close to their places of employment. Hell's Half Acre was the unfortunate name for a neighborhood that sprang up in the late nineteenth century around South Main, Washington and Thornton Streets. It got its name from the twenty-four-hour blast furnaces that were operated by the Akron Iron Company. The work was hard, and the workers, many of whom were Irish, were tough. Outsiders such as the Germans were not welcomed, and many a brawl took place in what was considered to be one of Akron's most dangerous neighborhoods. It was said that policemen never walked that beat alone. Despite the neighborhood's reputation, it was a thriving area where families lived and worked. After the factory burned in 1897, some moved to other parts of the city after taking jobs with other companies, including the rapidly growing rubber factories. Many stayed or moved a bit west, closer to St. Mary's Catholic Church, which would become an anchor for that neighborhood's Catholics, many of whom were Irish.

CHURCH LIFE

The first church to serve Akron's Irish was St. Vincent's, established in the 1830s as a mission visited by Father Basil Shorb, resident priest of the Catholic church in Doylestown, now Saints Peter and Paul Catholic Church. The first Mass was celebrated in 1835 by Father John Martin Henni from Cincinnati at the log cabin of well-known merchant James McAllister. By 1844, parishioners were attending Mass in a wood frame structure on Green Street, which served the parish until 1867, when today's church located at West Market and Maple Streets was dedicated. As the St. Vincent Parish grew, plans were made to construct a new church to serve Akron's Catholics who lived in the southern end of town, many of whom were Irish. In 1877, the first Mass was said at a building at Main and Bartges Streets, and in 1896, it became an official Catholic parish. The congregation grew quickly, and

Left: St. Vincent de Paul Catholic Church was founded in 1837 by Akron's early Irish. *Clifford B. Orr*.

Below: Before the current building at Thornton and Main Streets was dedicated in 1916, parishioners of St. Mary's Catholic Church met at this wood-frame building located on South Main. *Summit County Historical Society of Akron, Ohio*.

planning was soon underway to construct a new building. On the morning of Sunday, October 1, 1916, the bells of St. Mary's located at South Main and Thornton pealed before the church's grand dedication. For years, it served South Akron's Catholics, until it was closed as part of a restructuring plan by the Diocese of Cleveland. It was reopened in 2012 and serves what is now one of Akron's most diverse neighborhoods. As Akron's Irish Americans moved from the old neighborhoods to the newer parts of the city and the suburbs, many joined churches located in their home neighborhoods. St. Martha's, established in 1919, was the home parish for many Irish Catholics who lived in North Akron.

CLUBS AND ORGANIZATIONS

Life in Ireland remained difficult following the Potato Famine, and economic recovery was slow. Although proud to be American, Akron's Irish immigrants still cared deeply about Ireland and its struggles. The first Irish organizations established in Akron tended to be political, their missions devoted to helping the homeland. In 1880, Michael O'Neil and Isaac Dyas, founders of O'Neil & Dyas Dry Goods, donated one hundred dollars for the Akron Irish Relief Committee's drive to raise money for those who were suffering in Ireland. That same year, Akron's Irish established a chapter of the Irish Land League to raise funds to defray expenses for the defense of "agitators" who were fighting for reform of the British landlord system. When Ireland was struggling for its independence from Great Britain during 1919–21, Akron's Irish Americans mounted an aggressive relief campaign. The *Akron Beacon Journal* reported that thousands met at the Armory in April 1921 for a rally, and it was expected that twenty thousand tickets would be sold for a motion picture show benefit. Nearly every civic club and prominent businessmen, many of whom were not Irish, endorsed the campaign. In 1924, the Irish American Citizens Club was founded. A social club, it was open to all with "no religious dissension permitted."

Akron's chapters of the Ancient Order of Hibernians preserve and celebrate Irish culture today. It's unclear when Akron's first chapter was founded, but a Hibernian Society was mentioned in the *Summit County Beacon* in 1873. By 1913, there were three Ancient Order of Hibernians divisions in Summit County: No. 1 based in Akron, No. 2 in Barberton and No. 3 serving East Akron. The Akron ladies' auxiliary, chartered at the 1902 convention, was especially active in those early years holding picnics, dances and fish fry dinners at Young's Restaurant. In September 1915, it was reported that more than two thousand attended the annual Irish picnic at Springfield Lake. Curiously, the Hibernians' activities seem to have ceased by 1918.

In early 1953, a group of Irishmen rallied to re-establish a chapter of the Ancient Order of Hibernians. They met and planned for months at St. Bernard's Church and, by the fall of 1953, were granted a charter. Originally known as the Dublin Division, it was later renamed the Mark Heffernan Division after the group's first president. During their planning, it was discovered that the original charter still existed but was being used by a non-Irishman who used it in the 1940s to apply a liquor license for his "club," even listing fictitious Irish-sounding member names. A group of Hibernian members, including a police officer, paid the club a visit, retrieving the license and the charter. For the first few years, the members met at various church halls, usually St. John's on Brown Street. In the late 1950s, they moved into a building on Kenmore Boulevard, which included a spacious banquet room on the upper floor. For nearly fifty years, this location hosted St. Patrick's Day, All-Irish Day, wedding receptions and many an Irish wake.

Music is a part of any celebration, and the club has served as the venue for beloved groups like Irene Uhalley and the Irishmen, as well as Akron's Irish tenor Pat Flynn. There was never a dry eye in the house when Pat sang "Danny Boy." Accordion player Gordon Shaffer has been described as the godfather of Irish music in Akron, performing for more than fifty years and teaching Irish music to the children of club members. Long before audiences were swooning over Riverdance, Akron's Irish Americans were performing traditional Irish dance. In 1959, the club sponsored twenty-five young dancers in a competition in Cleveland. Soon they would be known as the Hibernian Irish Dancers. Since 1977, the Heffernan Division of AOH has sponsored a *feis* (Gaelic for festival), an annual event that includes a dance competition attracting upward of eight hundred contestants. The Margaret Judge Division Ladies Ancient Order of Hibernians, which shares space with the Mark Heffernan Division, caters most of the club's events. In 2007, Akron's AOH dedicated a modern new building on Brown Street where the singing, eating and celebrating continues.

In the 1990s, the St. Brendan Division and the Ladies Annie Moore Division were formed to serve folks in the northern part of the county. They met at the Moose Lodge in Cuyahoga Falls until buying a club room on North Main Street in 2006. For nearly twenty-five years, this group sponsored the annual Riverfront Irish Festival on Front Street in Cuyahoga Falls. The St. Brendan Division sold its North Main Street building in 2020, refocusing its mission on its charter motto of "Friendship, Unity and Christian Charity."

GETTING YOUR IRISH ON: ST. PATRICK'S DAY AND MORE

Akron's Irish were celebrating St. Patrick as early as the 1860s. In 1864, the *Summit County Beacon* announced that St. Vincent Church was holding a festival at Empire Hall to raise funds for building a church at Maple and Market Streets. Unlike today's revelries, the newspaper reported that this church-sponsored event was carried on with "the utmost decorum and good order." In 1873, Akron held its first St. Patrick's Day parade with a procession of bands and Irish clubs marching along South Howard, circling through downtown and ending with Mass at St. Bernard's Church. A grand banquet open to the public was held that evening at Sumner's Hall. By the 1880s, parades were no longer held; however, organizations and even businesses had begun to appropriate the day for nonreligious purposes. Merchants capitalized on the holiday, decorating their windows and selling green candy and other confections. In 1924, the elegant Portage Hotel served a dinner featuring roast Killarney duckling with County Kerry sauce and, of course, Potatoes O'Brien. It wasn't until 1980 that Akron's Hibernians resurrected the beloved annual tradition with a downtown procession, always held on the Saturday before March 17. Usually held at Summit Beach, the annual Irish Day picnic drew thousands each summer. According to the *Akron Beacon Journal*, twenty-five thousand Sons of Erin were expected at the 1941 celebration. A sensational advertisement invited guests to be thrilled as they watched the Great Marvelo "burn and bury alive pretty Miss Mickey O'Brien."

RESTAURANTS AND FOOD BUSINESSES

Unlike their Italian and Greek neighbors, Akron's early Irish were not known for establishing restaurants or food businesses. Irish food was to be had at home or enjoyed at picnics and other events sponsored by the

Walsh Brothers Lunch Room. Joseph and Harry Walsh got their start selling ice cream and newspapers at ball games from a horse-drawn wagon. In 1918, they opened this popular twenty-four-hour spot located at the corner of Main and West Exchange Streets. *Summit County Historical Society of Akron, Ohio.*

Irish immigrant Randall McAllister stands outside of his establishment, Louisville Liquor, located at 188 South Howard Street, circa 1887. His newspaper advertisements promised "to serve my friends and patrons with the finest old rye and bourbon whiskies." *Summit County Historical Society of Akron, Ohio.*

Hibernians. In the late 1950s, Akronites could trek to Macedonia to dine at Ray Kearns' Restaurant in the Round. A native of County Mayo, he and his wife, Myrtle, pulled out all the stops each St. Patrick's Day, when diners were promised "plenty of Irish wit, music, jigs, and cuisine." In the 1970s, a former funeral home director, Bill Quigley, opened Bridget's Bistro at 111 North Main Street. In 1983, it evolved into another Irish pub, Cavanaugh's, owned until 1995 by Karen Glinsek Davis, who named it after her mother's family. In the 1990s, Irish-born brothers and University of Akron soccer players Patrick and Derek Gaffney briefly operated Playwright's on Home Avenue. It boasted Guinness on tap and Irish specialties including Irish stew. There is no shortage today of eateries that celebrate on March 17, but few have true Irish roots. Named for the famous Notre Dame football coach Knute Rockne, Rockne's is always packed on St. Patrick's Day, despite the Norwegian heritage of its namesake. In the summer, Irish culture and heritage are celebrated at the annual summer Riverfront Irish Festival in Cuyahoga Falls, sponsored by the St. Brendan Division, and Taste of Ireland, a food and music event at Lock 3 Park organized by both of Akron's Hibernian chapters.

Hardworking and hard-living, from our city's earliest years, Akron's Irish made their mark on Akron's history. Some of our city's finest politicians, judges, lawyers, police officers and business owners trace their roots to Ireland. Whether your family hails from Ireland or you are Irish for one day in March, tip your hat to the Sons and Daughters of Erin who toiled on the canal, worked in our factories, founded businesses and brought their rich traditions to our city.

Bain taitneamh as do bheil!

Kathleen (Ward) Boyle

Kathleen grew up in Coaldale, Pennsylvania, where her father, John Ward, the son of Irish immigrants, worked in the mining industry for more than fifty years. In 1946, Kathleen and her new husband, John Boyle, also with Irish roots, moved from Pennsylvania to Barberton, where a job with Babcock & Wilcox awaited him. They remained in Barberton, raised four children and were active members of St. Augustine Church, home to the city's Irish Catholics. According to daughter-in-law Dianne Boyle, who married son John, many of Kathleen's favorite recipes were clipped from the *Catholic Universe Bulletin*. This family favorite, which is likely one of them, is still made and enjoyed today by her children and grandchildren. Dianne recalled fondly that Kathleen took great pride in the appearance of her dinner table, which always included a linen tablecloth, candles, glass salt and pepper shakers, a relish tray and small glasses of tomato juice. And of course, grace was said before every meal. Dianne and John keep their family's Irish heritage alive through their active membership with the Akron chapter of the Ancient Order of Hibernians. *Contributed by Kathleen's daughter-in-law Dianne M. Boyle.*

Lazy Day Stew

1 ½ pounds ground beef
Salt and pepper
1 large onion, thinly sliced
5 medium potatoes, pared and thinly sliced
1 (15-ounce) can peas, drained, liquid reserved
5 medium carrots, peeled and thinly sliced diagonally
1 (10½-ounce) can tomato soup
½ cup water

Season ground beef with salt and pepper. Spread in greased 2-quart casserole. Top with onions and potatoes. Spread peas over potatoes. Cover with carrots. Season vegetables as you add them. Combine pea liquid, tomato soup and water and pour over top. Cover and bake at 350 degrees for 1 ½ hours.

James "Jimmy" Mathews

Cavanaugh's Tavern on North Main Street was the place to be on St. Patrick's Day and during the "green season" leading up to it. Owner Karen Glinsek Davis served up her special corned beef sandwiches, and a pot of Jimmy Mathews's famous potato soup was simmering in the back. With the assistance of friends who helped to peel dozens of potatoes, Akron police officer Jimmy created a thick and comforting soup that was served until it was gone. A descendant of Irish immigrants, Jimmy had a love of cooking and food that led to his position as unofficial cook for the Fraternal Order of Police. He catered hundreds of events, including the annual Christmas party, one year making 1,200 cabbage rolls. He was also known for his sauerkraut balls and shared the recipe with *Akron Beacon Journal* food editor Jane Snow, who included it in a 1987 piece about Jimmy and his cooking. His recipes were also a regular feature in the monthly FOP newsletter, and the issue that included his potato soup recipe suggested, "It can easily be converted into an Irish seven-course dinner by serving one bowl of Cavanaugh's soup with a six pack of beer." Although Jimmy's original recipe includes carrots, Karen insisted that nothing orange could garnish his soup on St. Patrick's Day, as they were Irish Catholic, not Protestant. After retiring, Jimmy moved to South Carolina to be closer to his children and grandchildren, but he has fond memories of Akron and misses his large vegetable garden, where he grew hundreds of peppers and tomatoes, often sharing them with his pal Nick Anthe, who happily used them at his restaurant.

Cavanaugh's Potato Soup

6 to 8 cups chicken stock
1 large rib celery, split and diced
6 to 8 medium to large potatoes, peeled and diced
1 carrot, split and diced
1 medium onion, diced
2 scallions, chopped (white and green parts)
4 tablespoons butter
2 tablespoons or more flour
¼ cup or more milk
Minced ham (optional)
Salt and pepper

Add stock to a large stockpot and bring to a slow boil. Add celery and cook for 7 to 10 minutes. Add potatoes, carrot, onion, scallions and butter. Cover and cook for 35 to 40 minutes.

Mix flour and milk together and add to soup, adding more until desired thickness. Add minced ham, if desired.

Mark Eiffe and Karey DiSanto

A native Dubliner whose family roots extend back at least four generations in the Irish capital, Mark moved to Akron in 2018.

An Irish tradition is to have a family roast dinner on Sunday—all family members are expected to attend this weekly ritual. An essential and much-loved part of this dinner is the classic roast potato. We refer to them as roasties. They are so good and one of the first things that I cooked for my wife, Karey, to impress her. We have integrated them into family dinners here in Akron. The Sunday roast dinner ritual would start on Saturday when my mam, Esther, would go into Dublin City Center to Moore Street Market to buy fresh produce from the vendors. On Sunday morning she went to Mass, and my dad, Terry, would prep all the vegetables, leaving the cooking to Esther once she returned home. Customarily, the men would gather for a leisurely pint at the pub before dinner. Growing up, pubs closed between 2:00 and 4:00 p.m. on Sunday to support the tradition of family dinner.

Sunday Roast Potatoes

Canola oil (goose or duck fat is traditional)
Medium-size starchy potatoes (Idaho russets are perfect)
Salt and pepper
Parsley or other seasonings, to taste

Add ¼ inch of oil in the bottom of a 9 x 13 roasting pan and place in a 400-degree oven. Peel and quarter potatoes. Boil in salted water until only a small uncooked core remains. Drain and toss gently to roughen the surface. Make sure you've drained the potatoes well and patted them dry with a clean towel, as excess water can cause the hot oil to splatter. Carefully transfer the potatoes into the preheated pan. Baste the potatoes, ensuring they are coated with the hot oil. Periodically baste the potatoes during cooking. Roast until golden brown on the outside and soft on the inside. Test for doneness by inserting a fork into the center. Remove from the pan and season to taste with whatever tickles your fancy. We use sea salt, freshly ground black pepper and chopped fresh parsley.

Dave Kelly

Dave was born in Chester, England, to Irish-born parents Thomas and Margaret "Peggy" (Hickey) Kelly, both from Limerick. When Thomas joined the Royal Air Force, the family moved to various bases in England, as well as Germany and Hong Kong. As a young man, Dave's work as a project manager with a British engineering firm took him to the United States, where he met and married his wife and became a U.S. citizen in 2006. Because of his strong ties with his family living in England, he visits as often as possible. Dave describes his mother, Peggy, as "amazing" and completely devoted to her family. As she had eight children and a husband, her days were filled tending her garden, sewing, knitting, hand washing the family's clothing and, naturally, cooking. In her later years, Peggy spent her time looking after others, volunteering with her church and playing whist, a popular English card game. As she had to feed a family of ten, dinner, for the most part, was plain fare with affordable ingredients, often from Peggy's garden. She was known for her jams and pies made with berries that the Kelly children gathered along the roadside during the summer. A favorite everyday dinner was gammon with potatoes and cabbage, often made with vegetables grown by Peggy. Gammon is pork that has been smoked or cured, a cross between ham and bacon. Unlike ham, it must be cooked before being eaten.

Gammon with Potatoes and Cabbage

1 ½ pounds gammon or Virginia ham
2 pounds potatoes, new potatoes, if in season
1 head green cabbage, cored and quartered
2 tablespoons butter
Salt and pepper

To remove excess salt, place the gammon in a large saucepan, cover with cold water and bring to a boil. Drain, refill and boil for 5 minutes. Skim the froth from the surface. If still too salty, repeat the process. Reduce heat and simmer for about 1½ hours. Continue to skim any froth that rises to the surface.

Peel potatoes (if large, cut in half) and place in a large, covered saucepan. Cover with water and add a teaspoon of salt. Boil for 25 minutes or until the required firmness. If using new potatoes, there is no need to peel or cut. When cooked, remove gammon from the pot, reserving the liquid. Set aside and cover to keep warm while cooking the cabbage.

Bring gammon cooking water back to a boil. Add the cabbage and cook until tender, 3 or 4 minutes. Drain and return cabbage to the saucepan. Add butter, salt and pepper to taste. Cut and discard the rind from the gammon and slice into thick pieces. Serve with the buttered cabbage and potatoes. If using new potatoes, slather with butter and a little mint sauce.

Andrew J. Devany

My grandfather Dr. Andrew Devany was born in 1882 in the village of Dromore West, Sligo County, Ireland. He came to America in 1904 to attend Notre Dame University and went on to Northwestern University for his medical degree. He moved to Akron in 1912 as the in-house physician for the International Harvester Company, where he met and married his nurse, Beatrice Healy, also of Irish descent. They lived in a modest house on Dayton Street and raised a family of eight children: Mary Rose, Dan, Tom, Joe, Frank, Kathleen, Jack and Bebe. His office was at the corner of Main and Thornton Streets, which gave him quick access to downtown, where he served as the doctor for the Akron jail and the Children's Home. He continued to practice medicine well into his eighties, and the number of babies he delivered totals over three thousand. As the first highly educated Irishman in the city, he was initially subjected to anti-Catholic and anti-Irish prejudice. In the early 1920s, the Ku Klux Klan burned a cross on the family's front yard. Neighbors quickly set the Klan straight—Dr. Devany was off limits. He was one of the founding physicians of St. Thomas Hospital and, as an early supporter of Alcoholics Anonymous, was instrumental in establishing a treatment ward for alcoholics. A lifelong Notre Dame fan, he attended in 1935 what is considered the college football game of the century, Notre Dame's improbable comeback victory over highly favored Ohio State. Go Irish! This Devany family recipe is served with boiled vegetables (carrots, cabbage, onions), sandwich bread, cheese and mustard for a complete St. Paddy's feast. Contributed by Andrew's granddaughter Alice (Devany) Christie.

Corned Beef

This recipe is a family favorite, and even folks who don't like corned beef love it. Don't expect specific measurements for this recipe—it's more a description of the process. The only ingredients you need are one or more packages of corned beef, mustard (I use the cheapest yellow mustard I can find) and brown sugar. When shopping for your corned beef, try to choose ones that have little fat. Thinner beefs are usually preferable because they only have fat on the top, not an additional fat deposit in the middle as the thicker beefs do. First you simmer the corned beef or beefs (I usually make twelve for a large St. Patrick's Day party) in a large pot of water for about four hours or until a fork can be easily inserted. In the package with the meat, you usually find a packet of seasoning, which should be added to your pot of water. Make sure it is completely submerged in the simmering water. I place a brick on top of the meat. Be forewarned that the corned beef will shrink a lot during the cooking process so you may need more than you think. Next refrigerate the meat until it is cold enough to handle. Once cold you can easily cut off all of the fat, thinly slice the cold meat and place it standing up (like you are putting the piece of beef back together) in a metal or glass pan. Cover and refrigerate. This part of the process can be done a day or two in advance. Just before serving, preheat the oven to 350 degrees. Mix the yellow mustard with the brown sugar to make a thick glaze and generously cover the sliced corned beef with the mustard glaze. Heat in the oven about 20 minutes or until warm, and it's ready to serve. Leftover meat, if you have any, freezes well to be used later for sandwiches or corned beef hash.

Eileen (Toner) Yeager

Eighteen-year-old Eileen Toner of Castlecaulfield, County Tyrone, Northern Ireland, arrived at Ellis Island on March 15, 1913. The ship's passenger list recorded her as a "domestic" and her final destination as Washington, D.C. Although we don't know how or why she made her way to Akron, a 1918 *Akron Beacon Journal* society page snippet reported that Eileen and her sister, Betsy, of Washington, D.C., visited friends in Akron. Within six months of that visit, she married Ernest Yeager in a ceremony at St. Mary's Catholic Church. Granddaughter Marti has fond memories of her grandmother and her chocolate drop cookies:

My brothers, Ed and Jimmy, and I ran in the door of the house on Wymore Avenue in the Portage Lakes, ran past the squawking Conchita, my grandmother's African parrot, and down the stairs to the kitchen. In the kitchen stood my grandmother Eileen, a mock frown on her face, commanding us to "Stop!" The frown turned into a smile and her eyes began to twinkle. "Now, shurin what are you children wantin," she said in her Irish brogue. "COOKIES!" She would reach behind her, pick up the Mirro Aluminum Bun Warmer, take off the lid and reveal dozens of the most incredible dollops of heaven-on-earth: her chocolate drop cookies. To us, all under age ten, they looked to be the size of grapefruits. "Mind the crumbs, take those outside right now!" We would run to the tiny gazebo that faced the lake and devour them. My adult attempts to replicate the recipe have been less than successful. No matter, I can still taste them! Contributed by Eileen's granddaughter Marti Yeager.

Chocolate Drop Cookies

1 cup sugar
⅓ cup vegetable shortening
1 square baking chocolate, melted, or ⅓ cup cocoa powder
2 eggs, beaten
1 ⅓ cups pastry flour
1 teaspoon baking powder
½ teaspoon salt
1 teaspoon vanilla extract

Cream sugar, shortening and chocolate. Add eggs and beat thoroughly. Combine dry ingredients and add to sugar mixture, along with extract. Roll dough into walnut-size balls and place on a greased cookie sheet. Bake at 425 degrees for about 8 minutes.

Tom Gaffney

Tom Gaffney was 100 percent Irish. His father, Stephen, of County Roscommon, immigrated in 1903, first settling in Pennsylvania and later moving to Akron, where he took a job with Firestone. In 1922, he married Nora Walsh, daughter of Irish immigrants Patrick, of County Mayo, and Catherine (Conroy), of County Clare, both of whom arrived in the 1880s. Patrick, a rubber worker, and Catherine were married in Akron in 1897 at St. Vincent's Church. When Stephen and Nora moved their family to Dayton Street, their son Tom was only twelve. He was instantly smitten with Mary Lou Ringlein, the girl who lived across the street. They married in 1953 and were blessed with six children. Banoffee pie is a favorite family recipe that comes with a story:

> *Tom's Irish cousin, Finoula, and a friend set out to make banoffee pie one evening. After putting the pot and can of milk to boil, they went to have a good chat in the living room. The ladies laughed and talked, enjoying a wee bit of wine, completely forgetting about the dessert they were making, until…they heard an almighty bang and clatter! They rushed into the kitchen to find that the can of condensed milk had blown the top off the saucepan and exploded, spraying caramel everywhere. It took a while to clean up the mess, and for months Finoula found bits of caramel throughout the kitchen.*

Contributed by Tom's son, Michael Gaffney.

Banoffee Pie

1 9-inch prepared or homemade graham cracker pie crust (if you want to be traditional, replace graham crackers with digestive biscuits)
1 (14-ounce) can sweetened condensed milk
2 to 3 medium bananas, sliced

1 cup heavy whipping cream
1 tablespoon sugar
1 teaspoon vanilla extract
Chocolate shavings or mini chocolate chips

Place the unopened can of condensed milk in a saucepan. Fill the saucepan with enough water to completely cover the can of condensed milk. Bring to a boil. Maintain a slow boil for about 2 hours, checking frequently to ensure that the can is completely covered by water. Add more water, if necessary. Remove can with tongs, and let cool to slightly warm.

When the can has cooled to slightly warm, slice the bananas and place in one or two even layers on the bottom of the pie crust. Open the can of condensed milk, which will have turned a lovely caramel color, and pour it gently over the bananas, spreading to cover the bananas completely. Cover with plastic wrap and refrigerate until cold.

Whip cream with sugar and vanilla extract until stiff peaks form. Spread over the cold pie. Top with chocolate shavings or mini chocolate chips. Keep refrigerated.

Ellen "Eileen" (Hearne) Orban

Eileen was born in 1922 to William and Mary Hearne in Waterford, Ireland, on the same street where the famous crystal is made. As a young woman, she moved to London to live with her older sister Margaret. It was there that she met American serviceman John Orban, who was recovering from wounds he sustained during World War II. Eileen and John were married in London in 1945, but she didn't join him until a few months later. He was discharged and sent home to Akron, but she had to wait until her War Bride Act paperwork was in order. Several years later, they sponsored Eileen's sister Margaret and her husband, Bob Gunner, when they immigrated. For years, Eileen volunteered her cooking skills with the catering services of the Heffernan Division of the Hibernians, of which she was a longtime member. The *Akron Beacon Journal* featured a 1971 article about her and her famous trifle recipe. She was also tapped by Polsky's Department Store that year to teach an Irish cooking class for its "One World" bazaar to benefit the Akron Symphony Orchestra. Although her children didn't care much for it, Eileen often made this traditional Irish soda bread for her Irish and English friends and visitors. *Contributed by Eileen's daughter Sharon (Orban) Lofland.*

Soda Bread

3 cups raisins
3½ cups flour
½ teaspoon allspice
2 teaspoons cinnamon
1 teaspoon nutmeg
1 teaspoon salt
2 teaspoons baking soda
½ cup butter
1½ cups sugar
3 large eggs

Boil raisins in 2 cups of water until softened. Drain and reserve 1 cup of water. Mix flour, spices, salt and baking soda. Cream the butter and sugar. Add 1 cup of reserved raisin water and mix well. Add flour mixture and eggs to butter and sugar mixture and mix well. Fold in raisins. Place in a loaf pan and bake at 350 degrees for 1½ to 2 hours.

ITALIAN

Nick was born in Italy and came to Akron with his young wife in 1925. He worked in construction for twenty-five years. A faithful member of St. Anthony's Catholic Church and the Carovillese Club, he enjoyed working in his vegetable garden, playing bocce, and making wine with his own grapes. He always put his family first.

These words from a 2018 *Akron Beacon Journal* obituary could describe countless Italians who made Akron home. Family, work and tradition—these are the cornerstones of life and the threads that bind for Italian Americans.

WHERE THEY LIVED

Italians were later immigrants to Summit County. In the 1880 census, only 31 called Summit County home, with most living in Boston Township and Richfield. By 1910, the majority of the 800 who claimed Italy as their birthplace were young men. Although some were married, many were single and living as boarders in the vicinity of North Howard, Bluff, Furnace and Lods Streets. Most were unskilled laborers who worked in factories or for the railroads, but some operated shoe repair stores, bakeries, groceries and fruit stands. By 1920, the number of Italians living in Akron swelled to more than 3,600, with many working in the booming rubber industry. They came to Akron from all parts of Italy, but especially from the southern provinces of Campania, Calabria, Abruzzo and Sicily. Many came directly to Akron, while others spent time elsewhere before landing here, including, curiously, Krebs, Oklahoma, where a large number from Carovilli, Italy, went to work in the coal mining industry. When the mining industry in Krebs declined, some moved to cities where family members lived, including Akron. Dozens of emigrants from Carovilli moved from Krebs to Akron during the 1920s and 1930s, most settling on North Hill where the majority of Akron's Italian Americans lived. Not all lived in Akron's Little Italy, though. Many, especially those who worked in the rubber industry, settled near the factories where they worked, including a large number who lived in the neighborhoods around Grant Street.

CHURCH LIFE

Although most of Akron's Italians were devoutly Roman Catholic, they did not have their own church until 1931. In 1919, the *Akron Beacon Journal* reported that they would soon be able to worship in their own tongue when Father Alexander Yuppa arrived to establish a church for Akron's Italians. The new parish met at Holy Cross Polish Church on Lods Street until its building was constructed on Charles Street. A letter to the editor published a week later alerted readers to the fact that Father Yuppa was not a "real" Catholic priest but an apostate who broke away many years before. That church was never established, but soon the community began to plan for a parish to serve Akron's Italian Catholic families. In 1931, the Diocese of Cleveland sent Father Salvatore Marino to lead a congregation and oversee the construction of a new building. Nine years later, St. Anthony of Padua Church on Mosser Avenue was dedicated. Featuring marble from Carrara, Italy, it was built mostly by church members, many of whom were out of work due to the Depression. Meals to feed the workers came from church members, with women using their children's wagons to gather food from the neighborhood. A school was added in 1954, along with a convent for the Religious Teachers Filippini, the sisters who teach at the school. St. Martha's, founded in 1919 to serve St. Vincent parishioners who lived north of town, was also the home parish of many Italians. In 2009, it merged with Christ the King to form Blessed Trinity.

Not all of Akron's Italians were Roman Catholic, however. Some were members of the Italian Christian Church, which was rooted in the Pentecostal movement. Their first home, built in 1932, was on James Street, now part of the University of Akron campus. In the 1960s, the congregation changed its name to First Christian Assembly and moved to Riverside Drive in North Akron, where it was renamed Riverside Christian Assembly. Cornerstone Christian Assembly in Barberton is its successor.

CLUBS AND ORGANIZATIONS

With strong ties to their villages, Akron's Italian Americans organized clubs and benefit societies for fellow immigrants who shared the same heritage and traditions. Among the earliest were the Christopher Columbus Benefit Society, the Italian-American Republican Club and the First Italian Citizen's Club. In 1909, the three groups sponsored a state convention in Akron to promote October 12 as Columbus Day, an annual state holiday. Delegates from clubs across the state met to create a petition to present to the Ohio legislature, and it was adopted the following year. By the 1930s, Akron was home to more than thirty Italian American clubs and organizations, most of which were associated with the region from which its members came. In addition to offering support and benefits, they hosted card parties, raffles, cotillions, beauty pageants, wine-making and more. Every club held an annual summer picnic, usually at a location outside of the city such as Roma Park west of what is now Montrose, Orchard Lake Park at the intersection of Routes 8 and 303 or Brady Lake. Deeply patriotic, they held a strong interest in politics, and politicians wouldn't miss any opportunity to address an Italian American gathering or picnic during their campaigns. Republican presidential candidate William Howard Taft was the honored guest at Akron's 1908 Italian Ball. When Akron's Italian clubs formed the Council of Italian American Societies of Summit County in 1947, they agreed that it would make sense to merge the thirty-plus picnics into one celebration, the genesis of the annual Italian American Festival, which was held in Cuyahoga Falls until it moved in 2009 to Lock 3 Park in downtown Akron. Cuyahoga Falls continues to host Festa Italiana.

An early Italian club and one that remains active today is the Dante Alighieri Lodge 685 Sons of Italy, a chapter of the Order Sons of Italy in America. Organized in New York City in 1905, the Sons of Italy is the

Akron's Italian clubs were always well represented at the city's annual International Festival held on Main Street. 1978. *Akron Beacon Journal Collection, Summit Memory, Akron–Summit County Public Library.*

oldest Italian American fraternal organization in the United States. Akron's chapter, established in 1917, was open to anyone of Italian descent. Like most ethnic clubs, it didn't have its own home for many years, meeting in various lodge rooms of other clubs. In 1931, club members financed the construction of a new building located at Olive and Butler Streets in North Akron. Known as Columbus Hall, it featured a large lodge room and dance hall where they met and celebrated for many years. Today's club holds its meetings and events at various locations and focuses on providing scholarships and fundraising for charities, including for Cooley's Anemia, a disease associated with people of Mediterranean descent.

Those who came from Carovilli established the Societa di Mutuo Carovillese in 1925. Now known as the Carovillese Lodge and Club, its active membership sponsors Tuesday night pasta dinners, an annual sausage dinner dance, feast day celebrations, morra tournaments and weekly bocce games at its 1941 building on East Cuyahoga Falls Avenue.

In 1938, the Unione Abruzzese dedicated its new building on Tallmadge Avenue. The Italian-inspired stone building was constructed by its members, who contributed their old-world artisan skills to complete it. Until 2022, the

Italian Center member Tony Andriette serves up pasta at the club's weekly all-you-can-eat pasta dinners. *Akron Beacon Journal Collection, Summit Memory, Akron–Summit County Public Library.*

Castel di Sangro members enjoy a night at the club on East Cuyahoga Falls Avenue. *Castel di Sangro Collection, Akron–Summit County Public Library.*

Italian Center served as a community center, rental facility and home of its popular Thursday night pasta dinners.

Sicilians had their own club, Societa Siciliana Di Mutuo Soccorso, founded in 1933. They met at the Sicilian American Hall on Grant Street until 1956, when the group purchased a spacious brick estate on Theiss Road. Members of the Sicilian Club were the primary fundraisers for the Christopher Columbus bust placed at the Akron Municipal Airport in October 1938. The Sicilian-American Women's Club maintains an active membership, sponsoring tours to Italy, fundraising for local charities and selling cookies and pizza each year at Akron's Italian American Festival.

Started in 1938 by bootlegger turned bondsman Dick "Whisky Dick" Percoco, the Italian-American Professional and Businessmen's Club is one of the most active groups remaining in our city. Each year, the club hosts Viva La Panza (joy to the belly), a scholarship fundraiser that attracts upward of six hundred men. The tradition of measuring men with the biggest bellies is a highlight of the evening.

Other Italian American clubs that have come and gone include Unione Pugliese, Italian Democratic Club, Italian-American Republican Club, Italian Dramatic Club, Rositana Society, Marconi Club, Sons of Calabria, Combattenti Society and Castel di Sangro, one of the last to close in 1993. According to the Council of Italian American Societies website, fifteen clubs exist today.

RESTAURANTS AND FOOD BUSINESSES

Many of Akron's earliest Italian businesses were food-based. Most were mom-and-pop grocery stores located on the street level of their homes. In addition to the usual offerings of a neighborhood grocery, they also stocked traditional Italian ingredients for the home cook. Stores owned by Vitarella, Aulino, Pagano, Iacovazzi, Tisei and Ricciardi are listed as patrons in a 1926 *Akron Beacon Journal* advertisement to honor Columbus Day. Although many went out of business with the rise of chain groceries, some remained successful for many years. Nick and Maria Vitarella established one of the first, the Italian Terminal Market, first located at 54 North Main and later at Temple Square in North Hill. When Mel Todaro learned in 1959 that the business was for sale, he bought it, changing the name to Todaro's Imported Foods and expanding it to include catering. The party center he opened in

Frank Cianciola & Son. *Susan Macko Cianciola.*

1976 is run today by his son, Frank. Established in 1931, Frank Cianciola & Son was a respected grocer on Cuyahoga Street supplying Italian staples for your family meals. Although it was mostly wholesale in its later years, loyal customers who walked in to buy groceries were always welcomed. Their provolone was regarded as the best in town.

Still thriving after one hundred years, DiFeo's Poultry on Grant Street is known for its quality chicken and catering services. DeVitis Italian Market has been selling produce and Italian specialty products since 1952. Before locating to the current Tallmadge Avenue building, founder Frank DeVitis was a greengrocer in downtown Akron's Central Market. In addition to Italian products and ingredients, the house-made sausage, pasta sauces and Angelo's Heat and Eat products are especially popular. No Italian dinner is complete without bread and baked goods, and while many home cooks made their own bread and desserts, traditional cakes and pastries were offered by local Italian bakeries. Ninni's Bakery, which closed in 2013, was known for its Italian wedding cakes, traditional cookies and breads. Massoli's Italian Bakery on Brittain Road continues to make its traditional breads, which may be purchased at DeVitis or found on the tables of many local restaurants.

Who doesn't love a good Italian restaurant? Many of Akron's earliest restaurants were owned by Italian immigrants who brought their food traditions and cooking talents with them. Like early grocers, the first were

David, Robert and their father, Angelo DeVitis, at DeVitis and Sons Italian Market on East Tallmadge Avenue in 1977. *Akron Beacon Journal Collection, Summit Memory, Akron–Summit County Public Library.*

often operated from the downstairs of the owner's home, and most were located in North Akron. The earliest mention of an "Italian restaurant" in the *Akron Beacon Journal* was a 1919 classified advertisement for Paul and Angelina Mezzacapo's La Boheme restaurant at 204 North Howard

Street. The ad boasted of "famous national dishes prepared by Giuseppe Giordain and Tony Barra." In the 1920s, the Caruso Restaurant on Mill Street promised that its chef from Naples would prepare any dish you desire in "cheerful, quiet, and cool surroundings." A 1930s advertisement for the Garden of Italy Restaurant on Grant Street proclaimed that it had the only Italian beer garden in town. Akron's longest family-owned Italian restaurant was established in 1932 in the dining room of August and Eletta Iacomini's home on West Exchange Street. Called the Florentine Grille, it was the genesis of today's Papa Joe's, still operated by members of the family. Other restaurants that have stood the test of time are Emidio's, Dontino's, Rizzi's, Vaccaro's Trattoria and Parasson's. Beloved Italian restaurants that have come and gone include Casa Mimi, Sanginiti's, Gareri's, Dinardo's, Martini's and the Wine Merchant.

Pizza was introduced to Akron's diners later. Although which restaurant served pizza first is unknown, the first *Akron Beacon Journal* pizza advertisement appeared in 1939 for the Continental Restaurant and Bar located at 45 South Main Street. Three years later, the Kit Kat advertised "genuine Italian pizza—the talk of the town," and in 1951, Roma Pizzeria invited Akronites to "see genuine Italian pizza made by famous New York chef, Rocco Campanale." In 1953, Mario Caponi opened Rocco's, Akron's first carryout pizza shop, on the first floor of his family home and father Rocco's shoe repair shop on Thornton Street. In 1949, Nick Ciriello opened Luigi's at its current location on North Main Street. Although wonderful pizza parlors and carryouts can be found in neighborhoods throughout the city, Luigi's is the one that former Akronites must visit when they return to town. Lines out the door are not uncommon, regardless of the weather or day of the week.

Although fewer Akronites can claim to be 100 percent Italian today, Akron's Italian American community remains strong and vibrant. Its families, businesses, remaining clubs, spaghetti dinners, charitable giving and annual festivals will ensure that its place in the rich history of Akron's immigrants is not forgotten.

Buon Appetito!

Nancy (Ruggieri) Ciavarella

I was born and raised on North Hill, which probably meant you were Italian or knew someone who was Italian. My father was Angelo Ciavarella. He served in the army, loved to golf and, of course, loved his garden. I know that whose tomatoes were bigger was a topic of conversation on the golf course! My mother, Nancy, was an awesome cook, and everyone loved her cooking and baking. During Christmas and Easter, the basement was filled with baked goods, including nut and poppy seed rolls, pecan tassies, diaper cookies, Easter bread and lamb cakes…just to name a few. Every family I suppose had their version of wedding soup. I watched my mother make it, and now my children watch me. I always got my Swiss chard from my father's garden, but after he passed, I had to get it from the store. My soup would never be the same. Well, of course, I had to share my devastation on Facebook. Now all my friends and family keep me stocked! Contributed by Nancy's daughter Nancy (Ciavarella) King.

Italian Wedding Soup

½ pound ground beef (or a mix of ground beef and pork)
1 egg, slightly beaten
2 tablespoons Italian seasoned bread crumbs
2 tablespoons Parmesan cheese, plus additional for serving
½ teaspoon dried basil
1 teaspoon dried parsley
5¾ cups chicken broth
2 cups chopped escarole, spinach or Swiss chard
½ cup orzo pasta, uncooked
½ cup finely chopped onion
½ cup finely chopped carrot
½ cup finely chopped celery

In a medium bowl, combine meat, egg, bread crumbs, Parmesan cheese, basil and parsley. Shape into ¾-inch balls. Bake in 350-degree oven until brown. Drain off grease. In a large saucepan, heat broth to boiling. Stir in greens of choice, orzo, onion, carrots and celery. Reduce heat to medium. Cook at a slow boil for 10 minutes or until orzo is tender. Stir frequently to avoid sticking. Serve with additional Parmesan cheese sprinkled on top.

Caroline (Gentile) Lombardi

Caroline and her husband, Charles (Carmine), grew up in Opi, a small village in the Abruzzo region of Italy. They first settled in Wayne County and married there in 1897. By 1903, they were living in Akron on Furnace Street, where they operated a small grocery store until sometime in the 1920s, when Charles established a successful contracting and coal business. Caroline and Charles had eight children, including Leonard Anthony Lombardi, who served as a Summit County Common Pleas judge. Spitzad is one of Caroline's most beloved Lombardi family recipes and a favorite of her great-grandson David. Caroline passed the recipe on to David's mother, Peggy Lombardi, who has perfected it through trial and error, doing her best to cook the veal until, as Caroline instructed, "it is nice." For many years, it was served as a first course for the family's Easter dinner, followed by a beef dish known as braciola. Today, it is always served piping hot, with hard-crusted Italian bread and lots of finely grated Pecorino Romano cheese. The Spitzad is followed by a roast leg of lamb, mashed potatoes and other goodies. *Submitted by Caroline's great-grandson David Lombardi.*

Spitzad

3 large packages of round bone veal chops cut ½- to ¾-inch thick (approximately 3½ pounds)
3 to 4 (32-ounce) cans chicken broth
8 pounds endive, washed and cut into 2- to 3-inch pieces
10 to 12 eggs
½ pound medium-sharp Pecorino Romano cheese, finely grated
Pepper

Cut veal chops and brown in batches. Add chicken broth and cook until veal is tender (until it's nice!). Refrigerate overnight. Skim grease the following day. Bring the pot to high heat. Add endive and cook until tender. Beat eggs with 4 tablespoons of Romano cheese, and season with pepper. Pour eggs slowly over the endive and cook until set. Serve with Italian bread and sprinkle with powdery Romano cheese to taste.

Ezio Basile

Ezio was born in the northern Italian village of Idria to a Calabrian father, Vittorio, and Slovenian mother, Maria. After World War II, Ezio's family, along with the majority of Italians living in Idria, left their town, which was then under Yugoslavian rule. They moved to the city of Udine, Italy, where Ezio attended boarding school from the time he was a young boy. After losing his tailoring business, Vittorio made the decision to move the family to the United States, where he could start over and join his two brothers in Clarksburg, West Virginia, home to a large community of Italian immigrants. The family immigrated in 1951, and Vittorio found work as a tailor for a local store. Ezio graduated from West Virginia University with an engineering degree and was hired as a chemical engineer by B.F. Goodrich Chemical Division in Avon Lake. While vacationing with pals at a ranch in Wisconsin, he met Patricia Callahan of Milwaukee, who was there with college friends. After a few months of a mostly long-distance romance, the two married in 1959. In 1970, Ezio and Patricia moved to Akron, where they raised five sons and Ezio was employed by B.F. Goodrich. Their interest in historic preservation has led them to volunteer work with Progress Through Preservation and Cascade Locks Park Association, and Ezio was active with the Boy Scouts. They enjoy travel and return to Italy as often as they can. Jota is a traditional Northern Italian recipe heavily influenced by the cuisine of Germany and Austria and is especially popular in the city of Trieste. Ezio's mother, Maria, was an accomplished seamstress and excellent cook who shared her culinary skills with Patricia. Ezio has warm memories of his mother's jota.

Jota

1 ½ cups dry red kidney beans, picked over and rinsed
4 cups chicken stock
2 ham hocks
1 large onion, chopped
3 garlic cloves, minced
3 tablespoons yellow cornmeal
1 bay leaf
1 teaspoon dried sage
1 pound sauerkraut, rinsed and squeezed dry
1 pound red potatoes, quartered and cut crosswise into ½-inch pieces

⅓ cup minced parsley
Salt and pepper

Place beans in a bowl and cover with 5 cups of cold water. Let soak overnight. Drain. Place beans and 8 cups of water in a heavy kettle. Add stock, ham hocks, onion and garlic. Bring to a boil. Gradually whisk in cornmeal. Add bay leaf and sage. Simmer covered, stirring occasionally, for 2 hours. Remove ham hocks and place on a cutting board. Add sauerkraut and potatoes to bean mixture and simmer for 20 minutes, or until the potatoes are tender. Remove meat from ham hocks. Chop meat and add to soup along with parsley. Salt and pepper to taste. Discard bay leaf.

Louis Trocano

When Lenny Trocano was growing up, he thought that sausage hanging from your grandfather's basement ceiling was normal. Lenny's grandfather Louis Fred "Pa" Trocano was born in Cosenza, Calabria, Italy, in 1891. He and his brother Dominic immigrated to the United States in 1908, arriving through New Orleans and making their way to Chicago. The opportunity to work on the Lorain Carnegie Bridge (Hope Memorial Bridge) brought him to Cleveland, where he settled and met the much younger Filippa LaPorta "Ma," originally from Sicily. They were married in 1931 and had five children. The second oldest was Leonard, Lenny's dad. As newlyweds, Leonard and his new wife, Joanne (Hillegas), lived with them, and it was during this time that Pa passed the recipe on to Joanne. Every Sunday and holiday was spent at Pa and Ma's, and pasta was always on the menu. Pa's sauce was made with pork, usually neck bones, and his homemade sausage. Joanne taught her four boys how to make the family sauce, which continues to grace Trocano family tables today. *Contributed by Louis's grandson Lenny Trocano.*

Louis "Pa" Trocano's Family Sauce

2 pounds pork (ribs, neck bones or Italian sausage will do)
1 large onion, diced
3 tablespoons olive oil (you can only have too little olive oil)
3 cloves garlic, minced

2 (6-ounce) cans tomato paste
2 (28-ounce) cans tomato puree
2 (28-ounce) cans tomato sauce
4 tablespoons freshly grated Parmesan cheese
2 teaspoons dried oregano
2 teaspoons dried basil
2 teaspoons dried rosemary
Pinch cinnamon
28 ounces pasta cooking water
2 teaspoons salt
½ cup dry red Italian wine
12 tablespoons brown sugar

Bake pork at 350 degrees until fully cooked. Set pork aside and reserve drippings. In a large stockpot sauté onion in drippings and olive oil until soft. Add garlic. Stir 1 minute. Do not burn the garlic! Add tomato paste and continue to stir until it is hot and fully melded with the oil, about 2 minutes. Add puree and stir until hot, about 2 minutes. Add sauce and stir until hot, about 2 minutes. Add cheese, herbs, cinnamon and pork. Reduce heat and cook uncovered for 2–3 hours, stirring frequently. Do not burn the sauce. Add salt, wine and sugar to taste.

Let cool and refrigerate overnight. The next day, cook uncovered for an additional 2 to 3 hours. Remove bones and return any meat to pot. Before serving, add water from boiling pasta to thin sauce, as needed. Always mix the pasta and some sauce together in a bowl before serving. Add additional sauce as needed to taste.

Laura Salmon

Laura has been cooking since she was twelve years old and grew up in a large Italian family, where all celebratory meals included something Italian served at home or sometimes enjoyed at the family's favorite Italian restaurant, Papa Bear's in Canton. Her great-grandparents Dominic and Nunziata Russo came to this country in the mid- to late 1910s. Because Laura's mother typically served pasta sauce from a jar, Laura took it upon herself to re-create the sauces she remembered from her youth. This recipe is based on her memories, cookbook research and the recipes of Italian American mothers and grandmothers she has known over the years.

Bolognese Sauce

1 pound ground beef
1 pound ground pork
Salt and pepper
1 large onion
3 carrots
3 stalks celery
1 cup white wine (red works, too)
1 cup milk
1 (6-ounce) can tomato paste
6 tablespoons garlic, minced
2 (28-ounce) cans crushed tomatoes, plus ½ can of water per can to both rinse
out the can and add some needed water to the sauce
2 tablespoons dried oregano
Sugar

Heat a 6-quart or larger Dutch oven over medium-high heat until hot. Spray well with nonstick spray and immediately add ground beef and pork, browning thoroughly. Drain off about half of the fat, if desired. Season with salt and pepper to taste.

While ground beef is browning, puree the onion, carrots and celery in a blender or food processor until they are in very tiny bits. Do not drain the liquid.

Once the meat is browned, remove the meat and add vegetables. Cook over medium to medium-high heat until the liquid has evaporated and the vegetables have browned. Stir frequently. This may take up to 15 minutes or more. Salt to taste.

Add cooked meat and wine, stirring until the wine has completely evaporated. Repeat this procedure with the milk.

Reduce heat to medium and add tomato paste. Stir constantly until brown. Add garlic, tomatoes, water and oregano. Bring to a simmer. Reduce heat to low, cover and cook, stirring sauce every 10 minutes or so. Skim off the additional fat as it pools on the surface.

After the first hour, add salt and pepper to taste, adding more oregano and/or garlic, if desired. If the sauce is too acidic, add a teaspoon of sugar and simmer for another half hour before adjusting the seasoning and sugar levels. Continue to simmer for at least another hour and a half. Total cook time is about 3 hours.

Francesca (Pasqualino) Catalano

Francesca Pasqualino and Antonio Catalano were just teenagers when they came to Akron from Sicily in 1921—Francesca from Riesi and Antonio from Partanna. They met soon after arriving and, within a year, were married. During fifty-five years of marriage, they were blessed with five children and many grandchildren. Antonio retired from Goodyear, and both were active members of St. Paul's Catholic Church and the Sicilian Club. Francesca taught her girls how to cook at an early age, and her traditional Sunday spaghetti and meatball recipe was one of the first they learned. Now in her nineties, daughter Tina, who married fellow Italian American Leonard Filaseta, has been making it since she was eight or nine years old. It is still a family favorite and always served at Tina's on Christmas. *Submitted by Francesca and Antonio's daughter Tina (Catalano) Filaseta.*

Spaghetti and Meatballs

Meatballs
1 pound ground beef (or ground turkey)
4 cloves garlic, finely chopped
1 teaspoon fresh parsley, finely chopped
1 teaspoon grated Parmesan cheese
1 egg
½ cup dry bread crumbs
¼ cup white wine
½ teaspoon salt
½ teaspoon pepper

Sauce
1 pound pork neck bones
1 tablespoon olive oil
6 to 8 cloves garlic, chopped (not too fine)
1 (12-ounce) can tomato paste
1 (28-ounce) can crushed tomatoes
1 (28-ounce) can tomato sauce
3 leaves fresh basil
2 bay leaves
2 to 2½ cans of water
Salt and pepper to taste

Mix meatball ingredients together, but don't work it too long or the meatballs will not be tender. Form into balls, place on a cookie sheet and brown in 350-degree oven for 10 to 15 minutes, turning once. Do not bake them until fully cooked. They will finish cooking in the sauce.

In a large stockpot, sauté neck bones in olive oil until nice and brown. Add garlic and cook briefly. Do not let the garlic brown. Season with salt and pepper. Add remaining ingredients and simmer for 1 hour. Remove neck bones and simmer for an additional 1 to 2 hours. Season sauce with salt and pepper. As Tina's mother, Francesca, instructed, "When the sauce clings to the spoon, it's done." Add meatballs 10 to 15 minutes before the sauce is finished.

Anna Marie (Tiano) Teodosio

Family meals and holidays are special for Tom Teodosio and his Italian American family. They are a time for multiple generations to gather and celebrate their family and traditions. Many of those meals were prepared by his mother, Anna Marie (Tiano) Teodosio. A native of Derby, Connecticut, and the daughter of Italian immigrants, Joseph and Mary Tiano, Anna Marie met the love of her life, Alexander "Al" Teodosio, at a dance celebrating the end of World War II. After Al graduated from Brooklyn Law School, the two married, eventually moving to Akron, where Al joined his brother Ernest's law practice. Anna was devoted to her faith and her family, who gathered often at her home for holidays and traditional Sunday dinners. When she and Al celebrated their sixtieth anniversary in 2010, their children shared an announcement in the *Akron Beacon Journal* that included these words: "Thank you, Mom and Dad, for teaching us the meaning of love, commitment, and family." According to Anna's son Ninth District Appeals Court judge Tom Teodosio, Anna described meals like eggplant parmesan and pasta fagiole made with simple and cheap ingredients as "Depression dishes." Special dishes like lasagna and pasta dinners were reserved for Sundays and holidays. *Submitted by Anna's son Tom Teodosio.*

Eggplant Parmesan

2 small to medium eggplants
2 eggs, beaten
1 ½ cups seasoned dry bread crumbs

¼ cup olive oil
4 cups favorite spaghetti sauce
⅓ cup grated cheese

Peel eggplant (optional) and cut into ⅓-inch slices. Dip each eggplant slice into beaten eggs and then into bread crumbs.

Heat oil in a heavy skillet. Fry eggplant slices over medium-high heat, about 2 minutes per side, or until golden. Drain on paper towels.

Arrange half of the eggplant slices in the bottom of a baking dish sprayed lightly with nonstick spray. Spread half of the sauce over the eggplant. Sprinkle half of the cheese over the sauce. Repeat, ending with cheese. Bake at 350 degrees for 20 minutes or until cheese melts.

Sarafina "Sara" (Oliver) Triola

Sara Oliver was three years old when she and her mother, Mary, left their home in the village of Roccascalegna in the Abruzzo region of Italy to join her father, Michael, who came to Akron before them. By the time they arrived, Michael had bought a house on Wilbur Avenue and was employed by Firestone, where he would work for thirty-one years. Sara grew up in Firestone Park, and in 1953, she married Carl Triola, a son of Italian immigrants. In addition to raising their two children, Sara worked for O'Neil's department store for nearly ten years, sang in the choir at St. Paul's Catholic Church, was an active member of the St. Paul's Study Club and volunteered at Our Lady of the Elms School. According to her daughter Kathy, Sara, "who never knew a stranger," made almost daily trips to Joe Oriti's grocery on Cole Avenue, later Cox's Meats. When chatting one day with the new meat store owners, she complained that she was tired of making the same old things. They offered this take on city chicken, a popular dish of the time consisting of skewered cubed pork or veal. It is such a favorite that Kathy submitted the recipe many years ago for the St. Paul's Catholic Church cookbook. *Submitted by Sara's daughter Kathy (Triola) Boos.*

City Chicken Italian Style

2 pounds city chicken
I large onion, diced

2 medium green peppers, diced
1 clove garlic, minced
Salt and pepper
1 (8-ounce) bottle Wish-Bone Italian salad dressing

Arrange city chicken in a shallow baking pan. Top with onion, green pepper, garlic, salt and pepper. Shake salad dressing on top. Cover with foil and bake at 350 degrees for 1½ to 2 hours.

The Quattrocchi Family

One of the items on my post-retirement "To Do" list was to bring back some of the old family holiday baking recipes from my dad's side of the family. My Grandpa John was the son of Italian immigrants, Frank (Natale) and Margaret (Margherita) Quattrocchi, who owned a grocery store on West Bowery from the late 1890s until about 1930, and my Grandma Helen was the daughter of Hungarian immigrants, Peter and Susie (Zuzanna) Yetsko. There were so many recipes to choose from, including gorgeous nut rolls and a variety of delicious cookies, but this Sicilian horseshoe cookie recipe was first on my list. After Grandma died, my aunt Helen (Quattrocchi) Speelman took over making the cookies at Christmastime, sometimes enlisting the help of her younger sisters. As a young kid, I surreptitiously chose a place to sit at family gatherings closest to the big plate of horseshoes so I could eat them without anyone noticing… until I was caught and told, "Move away from the cookies!" During my college years, I ran across the well-worn handwritten copy of the recipe passed on to my mom, Eileen, and wrote a copy for myself. I first tried to bake them in 1977 but found it so daunting that I didn't try again until many decades later. Now that I have the time to make these, my eyes get a little misty with my first bite as fond memories of my family, especially those we've lost, come flooding back. In 2015, I was interviewed by Vivian Goodman for her WKSU show Quick Bites *about the horseshoe cookies, and in doing some research, I learned that the Sicilian name for these is "cucidate," meaning "little bracelets."* Contributed by John and Helen's granddaughter Dolli Quattrocchi Gold.

Horseshoe Cookies

Filling
½ pound walnuts or almonds
½ pound hazelnuts
3 (12-ounce) boxes raisins
¼ to ½ pound candied citrons
1 pound dried figs
½ cup sugar
2 cups water

Dough
3 pounds flour
1½ pounds sugar
3 tablespoons baking powder
Pinch of salt
1 pound lard
4 eggs, beaten
Water

Glaze and Decoration
Confectioners' sugar
Milk
Vanilla
Sugar sprinkles

Filling
Place nuts on a baking sheet and toast at 350 degrees for 8 to 10 minutes or until crisp, checking often. Grind the nuts, raisins, citrons and figs together, alternating them to keep the grinder from becoming clogged. Mix ground ingredients together and add sugar and water. Place in a saucepan and cook on medium for 20 minutes. If needed, add more water to keep the mixture from sticking to the bottom of the pan.

Dough
Mix all dough ingredients well, adding water to moisten, starting with ½ cup, until it's like pie dough. Roll dough to ⅛- to ¼-inch thickness. Use a water glass (family-style) or 3-inch cookie cutter to cut circles in

the dough. Place a rounded teaspoon of filling in a 1-inch strip across the top. Roll the cookie, sealing the ends and shaping into a curve with the seam on the bottom. Place on a cookie sheet and bake at 350–375 degrees for about 20 minutes. Cool before decorating.

Glaze

Make a loose icing out of confectioners' sugar, milk and a dash of vanilla, and add sprinkles for color.

Louisa Bologna

When Mary Gordon makes cannoli, she uses the stainless forms her father created to replicate those that belonged to her great-aunt Louisa Bologna. A native of Partanna, Sicily, Louisa and her husband, Joseph, came to Akron in 1911, where Joseph worked for Goodrich for many years. Joseph's sister Catherine (Bologna) Polefrone is Mary's maternal grandmother. Catherine and her husband, Philip, an immigrant from Cimina, Italy, came to Akron in 1905. They had nine children, and Mary's mother, Elizabeth, lived with them. From 1918 until about 1958, they owned and operated grocery stores on North Howard, Tallmadge Avenue and, finally, the North Hill Cash Grocery at 36 East Cuyahoga Falls Avenue, where they lived above the store. Mary remembers happy Christmas Days when all nine of Catherine and Philip's children and their families gathered in their upstairs home. Her grandmother, mother and aunts did all of the cooking, and Louisa's cannoli, a Sicilian specialty, was a treat everyone looked forward to. *Submitted by Louisa's grandniece Mary (Hill) Gordon.*

Cannoli

2 cups vegetable shortening
10 cups flour
¾ pound granulated sugar
1 cup white wine
½ cup or less milk
Vegetable oil for frying

Filling
3 (15-ounce) containers ricotta
½ cup or more sugar
4 cups chopped candied fruit
2 cups finely slivered dark chocolate

Cut shortening into flour until fine. Add sugar and white wine. Add milk as needed until dough is the consistency of pie dough. Cut into walnut-size pieces. Using cannoli rods, roll out each piece into a round, about ⅛-inch thick. Drop dough-wrapped rod into hot oil and fry until brown. Cool and remove from rods. Fill with prepared cannoli filling.

JOE RIZZI SR.

Joe Rizzi's passions were food and music. A native of Union City, New Jersey, he studied music at the Brooklyn Conservatory of Music and played accordion in the Navy Dance Band during World War II. In 1949, he formed the Joe Rizzi Trio, playing at venues along the East Coast. He opened his first restaurant in New London, Connecticut— the Blue Meadows—which featured live music, including his trio. In 1957, he and his wife, Marie Jo, and children moved to Akron and within two years started Rizzi Distributors, one of northeast Ohio's most respected restaurant supply and design companies. His first Akron-area restaurant, Rizzi's to Go at Fairlawn Plaza, opened in 1962, followed by locations on Waterloo Road, Wadsworth, Stow and Copley, where Rizzi's beloved pizza, pasta and Italian fried chicken are still served today. In 1990, he opened Rizzi's Ristorante, a fine-dining restaurant where the sounds of the Joe Rizzi Trio could be enjoyed three nights a week. According to family lore, this recipe was from a Rizzi's chef who trained at a culinary school in Italy. Although not a regular menu item, it was a frequent special and still a favorite of the Rizzi family. *Submitted by Joe's son Matt Rizzi.*

Double Chocolate Mousse Cake

All ingredients should be at room temperature.
1 pound butter
22 ounces chocolate chips, divided

1 cup half-and-half
1 cup sugar
1 teaspoon salt
1 tablespoon vanilla extract
8 eggs, lightly beaten
2 tablespoons margarine
3 tablespoons milk
2 tablespoons light corn syrup

Melt butter over low heat. Add 16 ounces chocolate chips, half-and-half, sugar, salt and vanilla extract. Stir until combined and melted. Slowly add eggs. Pour into 10- or 11-inch springform pan wrapped in foil.

Bake for 1 hour at 350 degrees. Cool to room temperature and release from the pan.

Combine remaining chocolate chips, margarine and milk over low heat. After all is melted, add corn syrup. Pour over the cake, letting it spread over the top and edges. Cover and refrigerate for 24 hours. When ready to serve, cut with a hot knife.

JEWISH

As a little boy in the 1930s, Bill Rogovy joined his Polish-born mother, Yetta, on her weekly trips to Wooster Avenue to buy chicken for Sabbath dinner. In search of the best bird, she would reach into crates of live chickens, selecting the plumpest for the next night's dinner. Bill's parents, Max and Yetta, were encouraged to come to Akron by family who told them about the many opportunities awaiting them in the booming city. Arriving in Akron about 1910, they made their home on Euclid Avenue in the heart of what would be, for many years, Akron's Jewish neighborhood.

Like Max and Yetta, most of Akron's Jewish immigrants arrived between 1880 and 1920, when more than three million Jews left eastern Europe, leaving behind anti-Semitism, poverty and persecution. The earliest to arrive were Germans and Hungarians, but many came from Russia, Poland and other eastern European countries. Among the first were Caufman Koch and Isaac Levi, who established Koch & Levi, Akron's first ready-to-wear men's clothing store. Established on Howard Street in 1848, it served Akron customers for 132 years. By the 1860s, Akron's Jews were working in the trades of clothing, meatpacking, liquor and various retail establishments. Many also worked as peddlers on Akron's streets, selling everything from rags and scrap iron to dry goods and produce. Abraham Polsky, the founder of Akron's beloved department store, got his start peddling on the streets of Akron. As they became more successful, some opened small stores, living above or behind their shops. Jewelry, salvage, produce, shoes, clothing and furniture businesses were often owned by Jews. Others opened grocery and specialty food stores with kosher butchers, delicatessens, bakeries and fish stores catering to the daily needs of Akron's Jews.

WHERE THEY LIVED

From the 1860s through about 1900, most Jewish families lived and worked in Akron's downtown commercial district and within walking distance of their Hebrew meeting place on Howard Street. As they became more affluent, many moved to the newly developing area around Wooster Avenue. By 1905, the Mirman, Cohen, Abramson and Wingerter families were living

A view of Wooster Avenue in 1946 when it was the commercial hub of Akron's Jewish community. Taken from the roof of Sam Bershon's Sahara Dry Beverage Company, the photo shows Joseph Sholiton's pharmacy and Nate Roseman's deli. *Akron Beacon Journal Collection, Summit Memory, Akron–Summit County Public Library.*

on Edgewood Avenue, and in another ten years, Jewish surnames would make up the majority of residential listings on and around Wooster. Jewish-owned businesses, including bakeries, butchers and grocers, thrived in the business district. East Akron was also home to a number of Jewish families during this time, many of whom owned businesses on East Market. By the 1930s, there was a shift to the area around Balch and Maple Streets and Copley Road, as well as Highland Square, where they were closer to the new Akron Jewish Center, which opened on Balch Street in 1929. A further shift west occurred in the 1960s and 1970s, when most of the remaining Jews living in the Wooster Avenue and Copley Road neighborhoods left for northwest Akron, and later Fairlawn and Bath, where the majority of Akron's Jews live today.

FAITH AND EDUCATION

Akron's earliest Jews practiced their faith devotedly, first meeting in private homes. In 1865, the small but growing community organized formally, establishing the Akron Hebrew Association, predecessor of today's Temple Israel. Over the next few decades, several more synagogues were formed to serve Akron's Orthodox, Conservative and Reform Jews, and temples were located in the neighborhoods where members lived, many of whom were often from the same country or spoke the same language. Beth El, organized in 1884 as Anshe Emeth, serves Akron's Conservative Jews. Russian Jews founded Sons of Peace in 1901. From the beginning, there was conflict, and a small group left in 1905 to form the New Hebrew Congregation. Hungarians attended Ahavas Zedek, and the Poles started Anshe Sfard.

Education and keeping their religious culture alive through their children were paramount to Akron's Jewish families. From 1909 until the early 1960s, many of Akron's Jewish children attended Talmud Torah at Wabash and Wooster Avenues or the Farband School until the two merged in 1955 to form United Community Talmud Torah. In 1965, Hillel Academy was opened, Akron's first Jewish day school. It is now known as Lippman School, in honor of longtime benefactors Jerome and Goldie Lippman.

As Jews left the old neighborhoods and young people adopted new ways of worship, most of Akron's early synagogues disbanded, their members joining what are today Temple Israel, Beth El and Anshe Sfard/Revere Road synagogues. Since the 1970s, Jews in the northern part of Summit County have met at Temple Beth Shalom in Hudson.

CLUBS AND ORGANIZATIONS

Close-knit and generous, Akron's early Jews took care of one another. Benevolent societies were formed to support the newly arrived, offering relief, healthcare, insurance and employment assistance. Since 1921, Anshe Sfard's Free Loan Society has offered small, interest-free loans to anyone in Akron's Jewish community to start or keep a business. The first loans were fifty dollars, considered enough for a peddler to buy a horse. Some groups were political, supporting workers and Jewish rights here and in other countries. Akron had chapters of Farband, also known as the Jewish National Workers Alliance, the Workmen's Circle and B'nai B'rith. The Workmen's Circle and B'nai B'rith are still active. Other groups include the Hakoah, Judean, Menorah, Chabad and Maccabee clubs. Akron's Jewish War Veterans Post 62 continues its work today by supporting the Brecksville Veterans Administration Hospital and conducting memorial services at each of Akron's Jewish cemeteries.

Jews were not welcomed by Akron's established country clubs. Wanting a place of their own, a group of prominent businessmen bought 117 acres of land in Montrose by selling bonds to members who became shareholders. Members were expected to make a donation to the Jewish Welfare Fund when they renewed their membership each year. Until closing in 2020, Rosemont Country Club was where Akron's Jews played golf, dined and socialized.

Akron's Jewish women have played no small part in the history of Akron's Jewish community. Although auxiliary groups were formed for men's clubs, and most synagogues have a sisterhood group, several charitable groups were established exclusively by women. In the 1860s, Akron's Jewish ladies were meeting as members of the Schwesterbund, an elite group of wives of Akron's Jewish leaders formed to help the needy. It is now Temple Israel's Sisterhood, one of Akron's oldest charitable organizations. In 1891, a small group of women formed the Daughters of Franz Joseph, now known as the Daughters of Israel. Hadassah, the Akron Chapter of Council of Jewish Women and Pioneer Women, now known as Na'Amat, focus their

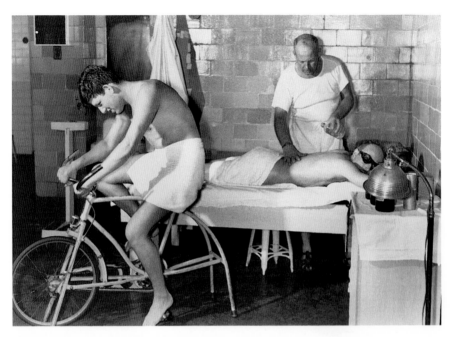

The Jewish Center on Balch Street included a health club where members could exercise and receive massages. *Jewish Community Board.*

fundraising efforts on supporting Akron's Jewish community and issues related to women, youth and the family.

Much of Akron's Jewish history can be told through the stories and growth of the Akron Jewish Community Center. When the Akron Jewish Center opened its new Balch Street building in 1929, Akron's Jews had a place to meet, socialize and even exercise. There was something for everyone—swimming, table tennis, fitness rooms and programs for all ages, toddler to elderly. It was especially popular as a hangout for teens, with many a romance kindled there. Eighteen-year-old Gloria Moss was new to Akron when she met her husband, Jack. A fellow Buchtel High School classmate invited her to the Center on a Sunday afternoon, when all the teens hung out. She told Gloria that there weren't a lot of boys, but "Jack Reich is there and he always dates the new girls." In 1956, the Center was the site of Akron's first Purim Ball, where young ladies were introduced to the community as Queen Esthers. Television star and Akron native Jesse White was the emcee that year. A theater guild put on plays starring local thespians, and educational programs were offered by what would become the Akron Jewish Civic Forum. Eleanor Roosevelt, Will Rogers, Margaret

Sonia Allison was the resident cook of the Akron Jewish Center for twenty-five years. This 1948 photo shows her and other women preparing food in the Center's kosher kitchen. *Jewish Community Board Collection, Summit Memory, Akron–Summit County Public Library.*

Bourke-White, Amelia Earhart, Bertrand Russell and Edward R. Murrow were among the featured speakers. In 1957, the Women's Auxiliary held its first annual Women's Day, offering an elegant luncheon and an array of programs with a theme of "What every woman wants to know." Topics that year included how to be a perfect hostess, dealing with your teenager, public speaking, antiques and houseplant care. Keeping everyone informed was the center's newspaper started in 1929, the *Akron Jewish Observer*, now the *Akron Jewish News*.

Plans for a modern new center began in 1958 when land on White Pond Drive was purchased. A recreation center and day camp building was dedicated in 1962, and the new Center headquarters was built in 1973. Known as the Schultz Campus for Jewish Life, it includes the Shaw Jewish Community Center, Lippman School, Mandel Early Childhood Education Center, Jewish Family Service, Schultz Towers and Beth El Synagogue. It also serves as home for the Jewish Community Board of Akron.

RESTAURANTS AND FOOD BUSINESSES

When a group of Jewish elders came together in 2003 for an oral history project, the conversation soon turned to food. Everyone had opinions about the best Jewish bakery, kosher butcher or fish store, sharing memories of shopping at the many Jewish-owned businesses on Wooster Avenue. Long before Wooster Avenue, however, Akron's early Jews patronized the peddlers who drove their horse-drawn carts through Akron's streets selling produce, meat, eggs and fish to neighborhood housewives. Some, like butcher David Leopold, would open their own shops. From the 1860s until his death in 1923, he was one of Akron's most respected butchers. By the 1890s, kosher meats could be bought from the city's first kosher meat market owned by a Russian immigrant, Elias Luntz. Soon, Akron would have its first kosher delicatessens, some with sit-down service. A favorite was Beck's, opened in 1912 by Austrian immigrant Jacob Beck. Beck's was famous for its paprikash, charcoal-broiled steaks and pickles, home-canned by his wife, Regina. Jacob Beck loved the theater and became a promoter, bringing Yiddish drama and musicals to Akron's Jews—tickets sold from his deli, of course. Moskovitz's was another beloved deli opened in 1916 by Harry Moskovitz. For forty-two years, it was the place for Akron's best borscht, gefilte fish, matzoh ball soup and dark pumpernickel bread. Schneier's Fish and Oyster Market on North Howard was opened by Russian immigrant brothers Max and George Schneier, who expanded the business to a wholesale operation, changing the name to Schneier Finer Foods.

As Akron Jews made the Wooster Avenue area their home, Jewish-owned businesses followed. From the 1920s through the 1960s, Jews could do all of their Sabbath shopping without leaving their neighborhood. William Stile and Jack Saferstein's grocery stores were the places for your everyday needs; Morris Munitz and Hyman Daly sold kosher meats; and the freshest kosher poultry could be found at Akron Poultry, owned by Herman Wollins, also a well-known local boxing promoter. The finest fish in the neighborhood were found at Mintz's or Stein Fish, and shoppers had their choice of the New York Bakery or the Pittsburgh Bakery for fresh bread and pastries. Roseman's Delicatessen, operated by Nate Roseman, was famous for its "jumbo kosher French popped frankfurter with famous mystery relish." Not fried, grilled or broiled, the never-to-be-revealed secret cooking method produced what Mr. Roseman called the "thoroughbred of hot dogs."

A favorite lunch spot of local politicians, Roseman's Deli was known for its hot corned beef sandwiches "fit for a king" and kosher hot dogs with special sauce. *Jewish Community Board.*

As Akron's Jewish families moved even farther west, so did their food businesses. By the 1950s and 1960s, many of the old Wooster Avenue businesses had closed or moved to Copley Road. Ronald Wolf's Nosh-A-Rye Deli, first located on Copley Road and later at Wallhaven, was known for its corned beef and "fresh Cleveland baked goods." As late as the 1970s, Sam Segal and Oscar Nagel ran kosher markets on Copley, just a few doors from each other. Not far away was the Wildwood Bakery. When founding owner Carl Zschech retired in 1947, Joe Dunn took over and ran it until 1975, when twenty-three-year-old Mark Goldstein and his younger brother Steve bought it, keeping it alive for another five years. Beloved by Jews and non-Jews alike, Lou & Hy's on West Market was Akron's best-known Jewish deli, famous for its sky-high sandwiches, authentic New York cheesecake and bowls of pickles on each table. It was started in 1965 by brothers-in-law Lou Kay and Hy Potrock and later managed by Lou's son, Alan, until the landmark deli closed in 1998.

JEWISH FOOD AT HOME

For Beverly "Bunny" Magilavy Rose, the most important Jewish holiday took place every week. Friday Sabbath dinner was always special, a time to gather with family, honor their faith and share a traditional meal. Dressed in their Sabbath best, they sat down to a beautifully set table with the family's better china and often a centerpiece. According to Bunny, "presentation was everything." At least three courses were served, often matzoh ball soup, chicken, brisket or stuffed cabbage, and always challah and wine. One of her grandmother's delicious desserts topped it off. The high holidays of Rosh Hashanah and Yom Kippur were celebrated more lavishly, with even more dishes. She especially looked forward to Passover because the celebration often included her aunts, uncles and cousins.

Although Akron's Jews don't trek to Wooster Avenue to buy ingredients for Sabbath dinner, and some no longer adhere to kosher rules, they continue to hold their food traditions close. Families still gather to observe holidays; family recipes are savored and shared, honoring those who are no longer with them.

Es Gezunterheyt!

Brian Barnett and Beverly (Gergel) Barnett

When Beverly Gergel's father, Isadore, welcomed World War II soldiers stationed at Fort Jackson to his home and synagogue in Columbia, South Carolina, he didn't expect that three of his four daughters would meet and marry boys from Summit County. James Barnett of Barberton married Beverly, and Marvin (Buddy) Wein of Akron married her younger sister Cynthia. After the war, both couples moved to Akron, soon to be followed by their youngest sister, Maxine, who would also fall in love with and marry an Akron boy, David Schneir. The sisters learned to cook traditional Jewish foods from their mother, Ida, a Polish immigrant who met Russian immigrant Isadore after settling in Columbia. Isadore joked that there were three women of marrying age when he arrived. One was too tall, one was cross-eyed and then there was Ida. They married in 1920. An iconic eastern European recipe, gefilte fish uses ingredients that were accessible even for the poorest Jews, and the fish they used was kosher and cheap. Now living in Omaha, Nebraska, Ida's grandson Brian Barnett fondly remembers sitting in her Columbia kitchen as a young boy picking fish from the bones under her watchful eye. Not a morsel was wasted. She would chop the fish until it was, in her words, the "consistency of a cloud." Her gefilte fish recipe and others from Ida and other members of the family were compiled by Ida's granddaughter Sheryl Wein Ryckebush for a family cookbook, *Gergel's Goodies*.

Ga-Ma's Gefilte Fish and Horseradish

Fish Broth
Fish heads and bones
¼ pound carrots, chopped into ¼-inch pieces
1 onion, sliced
2 stalks celery, diced into ¼-inch pieces
Water
Salt to taste

Fish Balls
2 pounds whole whitefish
2 pounds whole pike or pickerel
3 eggs

Salt
Pepper
1 tablespoon oil
2 medium onions, sliced
Carrots, sliced to ¼-inch thickness
Paprika

Broth: Fillet fish, reserving heads and bones for fish broth. Place all fish broth ingredients in stock pot, cover with 1 inch of water and simmer for one hour. Strain.

Fish balls: Grind boned fish with onion and put in chopping bowl. Add eggs, salt and pepper. Chop together, adding small amounts of cold water—just enough until it feels light and fluffy. Add oil and chop again. Form into balls.

Place sliced onion and carrots in roasting pan and add ¼ inch of fish broth. Lay fish balls on top and sprinkle lightly with paprika. Cover and bring to a boil. Reduce heat to medium low to medium heat so it bubbles gently. Cook for 2 hours, adding more broth, as needed. If you run out of fish broth, chicken broth works fine. Uncover and cook an additional 60 to 90 minutes, basting frequently. Fish should be beautifully glazed. Place balls on a platter, topping each with a slice of carrot. Cover and refrigerate. Serve cold or at room temperature with horseradish.

Horseradish

½ pound fresh horseradish root
2 tablespoons canned or fresh boiled beets, chopped
1 tablespoon white vinegar
1 ½ teaspoons sugar

Grate horseradish into a bowl. Add beets (with juice), vinegar and sugar. Place into a tightly sealed jar and let rest for at least 2 hours before serving. Will keep in the refrigerator for up to 3 months. Do not freeze.

Leona (Magilavy) Sacks

Leona was born in Akron in 1916 and grew up on Clark Street, not far from her father Daniel's East Market Street men's apparel business, Danny's Inc. Daniel Magilavy emigrated in 1905 from Grodno, Poland, and in 1914 married Belle Kuttner, who had emigrated with her family from Chlevestia, Romania. Along with their five children, Daniel and Belle's household included Belle's mother, brother Adolf and Daniel's father. A Central High graduate, Leona was active in the Akron Jewish Center from the time she was a teen, serving on various committees and boards and organizing special events. It was at one of these events that she met her husband, Sidney Sacks, whom she married in 1941. After Sidney returned from his service in the Navy during World War II, he joined his family's business, Sacks Electric, where he worked for fifty-five years. Leona and Sidney were pillars of Akron's Jewish community, and both were active members of the Jewish Center and Temple Israel, where Leona served as the first woman president. Leona was also a proud and devoted volunteer for the Red Cross, where, in 1941, she began her service as a first aid instructor. According to Leona's son Michael, whose wife, Bobby, is the keeper of the recipe, Leona's chopped herring likely dates to the early 1900s or possibly earlier, when everything would have been grated by hand. "It is sweeter than regular or creamed herring and has a fuller consistency; however, you still need to like the taste of herring to enjoy this dish." *Contributed by Leona's daughter-in-law Bobby (Katz) Sacks.*

Chopped Herring

3 (20-ounce) jars herring in wine sauce, drained. Discard onions.
1 loaf challah, crusts trimmed and cut into large cubes
6 to 8 apples, peeled, cored and roughly chopped
8 hard-boiled eggs, roughly chopped
1 onion, roughly chopped
1 tablespoon sugar
½ cup chopped red pepper

Mix herring, challah, apples, eggs, onion and sugar. Working in batches, place in food processor and process until mixture reaches a spreadable but slightly chunky consistency. Place mixture in a bowl and add red pepper.

Elsie (Robins) Reaven

Elsie was born in Cleveland in 1921 to Rachel (Civin) and Boris Robins but grew up in Denver's National Home for Jewish Children, where she and her older sister Pat were sent following the death of their mother from tuberculosis when Elsie was just seven years old. At the time, Denver was a destination for TB patients seeking fresh air and treatments offered by the National Jewish Hospital and the Jewish Consumptives Relief Society. When Elsie graduated from high school, she left Denver and joined Pat, who had settled in Chicago. In 1945, Elsie moved to Akron, took a job as an air traffic controller at the municipal airport and soon met Sidney Reaven, a young law school student and the son of Russian immigrants, Israel and Lena. Elsie and Sidney married and raised their four children in Akron. From the time she arrived, Elsie involved herself in politics and community welfare issues and, in her forties, went to Kent State, where she received a master's degree in political science. She served for several years as Akron's First Ward councilperson and was the first woman elected to the city council as an at-large candidate. She served at large for another six years. She also served as executive secretary of the Summit County Democratic Party. Elsie was an advocate for fair housing (taking her daughter Deborah to picket when she was fourteen) and abortion rights, receiving national attention in 1978 when the controversial abortion laws passed by Akron City Council were struck down by the United States Supreme Court. She left the council when she and Sidney moved to San Francisco to be closer to their children but really to their grandchildren. At every Jewish holiday, Elsie contributed wonderful food, including this delicious dish. She gave her Foley's food mill to daughter Deborah when she passed on the job of making the chopped liver. *Contributed by Elsie's daughter Deborah (Reaven) Lopez.*

Chopped Chicken Livers

¼ to ½ cup butter or schmaltz
1 pound chicken livers (if cooking more, use same ratios)
½ sweet or yellow onion, halved and sliced
Red wine (optional)
1 hard-boiled egg, chopped (or more as desired)
1 stalk celery, chopped

Salt and pepper

Place ¼ to ½ cup of schmaltz or butter in a covered baking dish. Add livers and onions in layers with onions on top and bottom. Add a bit of wine, if desired.

Cover and bake at 350 degrees for 30 to 45 minutes or until livers are tender and onions are cooked.

Put livers and onions through a food mill or food processor and process until still chunky. Add additional melted butter or schmaltz as needed until it looks/feels/tastes good. Add egg and celery, and salt and pepper to taste. Refrigerate for at least I hour. Mix and mold or serve.

Bessie (Olitsky) Omansky

Lois Reaven's family arrived in Akron more than a century ago. Her father, William Rubenstein of Wlodawa, Poland, came in 1910 with his parents, David and Taube (Thelma). According to Lois, her grandfather David first worked as a peddler, selling produce from a pushcart. Her father, William, aspired to do better and started his own company, Akron Terminal Produce, which he owned for more than twenty years before taking the position of produce buyer for Betsy Ross Foods. Her mother, Rose, was born in Philadelphia to Louis and Bessie (Olitsky) Omansky, who had emigrated just a few years before from Odessa, Russia. By 1910, Louis and Bessie had made their way to Akron, where they operated the Akron Kosher Meat Company on Bowery Street just across the street from their synagogue, Sons of Peace. They lived on State Street, close enough that Louis could walk back and forth between his home and store. In addition to raising five children, helping Louis in the shop and serving on the ladies' auxiliary of Sons of Peace, Lois's Bubby Bessie found time to share her recipes for traditional Jewish dishes with the *Akron Beacon Journal.* In 1936, food writer Glenna Snow described her as "one of our best contributors, especially where Jewish dishes are concerned." Called *shchi* in Russia, this traditional soup is still a favorite of Lois's family. *Contributed by Bessie's granddaughter Lois (Rubenstein) Reaven.*

Bubby's Cabbage Soup

3 pounds beef short ribs
1 medium head cabbage, coarsely shredded or grated
1 (14½-ounce) can sauerkraut
1 (14½-ounce) can tomatoes, drained and rinsed twice
1 large onion, slashed in the middle, but not cut all the way through
2 teaspoons (or more) brown sugar
2 teaspoons (or more) lemon juice
Salt to taste

Combine all ingredients and bring to a boil. Reduce heat and simmer, covered, for about 4 hours. Salt to taste. Add additional brown sugar and lemon juice, as desired. Freezes well.

Rita (Sill) Solitt

Rita grew up surrounded by love in the Cleveland home of her Russian immigrant grandparents Morris and Sophie Gordon. It was a large house—big enough for Rita and her single mother, Mary (Sill), and all of her aunts and uncles who lived with them, even after they married. Morris Gordon was a WPA stonemason who worked on several of Cleveland's municipal buildings, some of which still stand today. Her mother, Mary, worked at Wilbur-Rogers Ladies Apparel in downtown Cleveland. According to Rita, her grandmother Sophie, who was "very enterprising," started a bottle business where she and a friend collected bottles and redeemed them for cash. Rita remembers visiting her grandmother's shop on East 105th Street where all of the bottles were stored and how she had to keep her elbows to her side to avoid a disastrous crash of glass. Rita loved her grandmother, who "was a darling, so sweet," and remembers great fun with her uncles, who always played with her. She recalls with fondness her grandparents' dining room and dinner with her large extended family. Because it could feed a crowd, brisket was often on the menu. When Rita made it for her own family, she always asked the butcher for the largest brisket, and depending on the size, sometimes she had to recruit someone to take it in and out of the oven. Rita now lives in Akron, where she settled after marrying Sam Solitt, who was in the jewelry business and top salesman for Keepsake Diamonds, a brand of high-quality diamonds sold throughout the country.

Beef Brisket

5- to 6-pound single-cut choice beef brisket
2 teaspoons salt
1 teaspoon pepper
1 teaspoon paprika
2 to 3 cloves garlic, smashed
2 large yellow onions, sliced
3 carrots, cut into 2- to 3-inch pieces
1 cup catsup
½ cup white vinegar
¾ cup brown sugar
½ cup water

Season brisket with salt, pepper and paprika. Cover bottom of roasting pan with garlic, onions and carrots. Place seasoned brisket on top.

Combine catsup, vinegar, brown sugar and water. Pour over brisket. Cover and roast at 325 degrees—35 to 40 minutes per pound. Remove from oven and let cool. Once it is cooled, place it in the refrigerator for a few hours. Slice and return to refrigerator. Reheat the next day at 325 degrees for 45 to 60 minutes.

Celia (Lifshitz) Newman

Celia was eight years old in 1921 when she and her mother, Nadia; brother, Jack; and sister, Martha, fled their home in Ekaterinoslav, Russia, for the Polish border. In a 1965 *Akron Beacon Journal* article, Celia recalled their escape hidden under a pile of hay on a farmer's wagon: "Bolshevik soldiers guarded the border....They prodded every hay load leaving the city with long sharp poles....My mother stuffed handkerchiefs in our mouths, telling us not to cry out." Although they made it safely to Warsaw, their immigration to the United States was held up because their husband and father, Meyer Lifshitz, who was living in Akron, had not completed his citizenship. Meyer appealed to his friend and business associate C.L. Knight for help. A U.S. congressman at the time, Knight signed the family's visa, and the family was reunited. Celia and her family made their home in Akron, where Meyer founded the Portage Insurance Agency and established himself as a leader of Akron's Jewish community. A few years after graduating from West High, Celia met Abe Newman of Louisville, Kentucky, whose family also fled Russia in 1921. They became engaged, and a wedding was scheduled for June 1938, but Abe, who was living in Atlanta, didn't want to wait any longer to be with his beloved, Celia, or spend any more money on long-distance phone charges. Ten days before their scheduled nuptials, he made an early morning call to Celia, begging her to get on the next plane so they could marry immediately. Celia had never been on a plane and was hesitant at first, but she excitedly boarded a morning flight. She arrived at 2:30 p.m., and they were married at the courthouse an hour later. Celia and Abe eventually moved to Akron, where they raised their son, Herb, and daughter, Florence (Newman) Becker, and were members of Beth El, Rosemont Country Club and the Akron Jewish Center. Celia's daughter-in-law, Dianne Newman, shared that Celia, "who wasn't much of a cook," claimed that her marriage license didn't include anything about cooking and cleaning. The origin of Celia's cabbage roll recipe is not certain, but Dianne and her sister-in-law, Florence, agree that it is most likely from Celia's mother, Nadia Lifshitz Govendo, or possibly her sister, Martha (Lifshitz) Kodish Winer. *Contributed by Celia's daughter-in-law, Dianne (Rubin) Newman.*

Hungarian-Style Stuffed Cabbage

Cabbage and Filling
2 medium heads cabbage
2 pounds ground chuck
1 cup Rice Krispies or cooked rice
1 large onion, grated
Salt and pepper
1 clove garlic, crushed
1 tablespoon chicken fat (optional)
½ cup bread crumbs

Sauce
1 (28-ounce) can crushed tomatoes
1 (10-ounce) can beef bouillon
½ cup white raisins
Salt and pepper
1 cup water

1 large onion, diced
Juice of 1 ½ large lemons
6 to 8 gingersnaps, broken
½ cup dark brown sugar
Sauerkraut (optional)

Core and freeze cabbage heads. When ready to use, defrost and peel away—the leaves will be just right for rolling. Combine filling ingredients. In a separate bowl, combine sauce ingredients. Place a well-rounded tablespoon of the filling mixture on the thick part of the leaf. Roll once, fold one end in and continue to roll, folding in the other end.

Place rolls in a large pot or Dutch oven and cover with sauce and sauerkraut, if desired. Cover and simmer for at least 2 hours or longer if you have more than 20 rolls.

Dora (Hahn) Friedman

Every Friday, our family kitchen was the scene of my grandmother's genius realized. Always challah, always a kuchen and often, kipfel, strudel (apple, cherry, poppyseed, cheese), nut tortes, puff pastry and more. We lived together during World War II, and when my dad returned, we bought a duplex and continued living together. For me and my siblings, Nicki and Dan, it was a wonderful growing up. My grandparents were immigrants, coming here before World War I from all parts of the Austro-Hungarian Empire. My maternal grandmother, Dora Hahn, was born in 1889 in Bonyhad, Hungary, where her parents, Simon and Josephine, owned a small vineyard. After her father died, Dora's brother Sigmund, a successful Pittsburgh businessman, helped the family immigrate to the United States in 1905. Only one sister remained in Hungary. Grandma Dora met my grandpa, Louis Friedman, through friends in Cleveland. They were married and came to Akron, where my grandpa lived and worked with his brother. They were in the taproom business, owning Holland Mill Tap Room and Falls Tap Room. My grandparents Dora and Louis had two daughters, my mother, Eleanor (Ellie), who married my dad, Jack Magilavy, and Beatrice, who married Louis Silverberg. Jewish recipes all originated, I think, for various family and religious occasions. It is hard to say who originated a particular dish because each cook added her own special ingredients, seasonings and flavorings. For example, after a Jewish funeral, the family and close friends gather at the family's home for a meal bought and prepared by close friends. A sweet kugel was often part of the menu. This recipe is a family favorite and a specialty of my mother, Ellie. Cooking in our family, as in many others, was considered an art. It was and still is a significant part of our lives. Contributed by Beverly (Magilavy) Rose.

Ellie's Sweet Noodle Kugel

8 ounces cream cheese
4 eggs, beaten
1 cup sour cream
4 tablespoons butter, melted
½ cup sugar
1 (12-ounce) package wide noodles, cooked
Apricot preserves
½ cup white raisins

Topping
1 cup cornflakes
2 tablespoons sugar
1 teaspoon cinnamon
¼ cup melted butter

Mix cream cheese, eggs, sour cream, butter and sugar. Toss with cooked noodles. Place one half of noodles in 9 x 13 glass baking dish. Top with 6 to 8 teaspoons of preserves and half of raisins. Repeat. Cover with plastic wrap and refrigerate overnight. Before baking, mix topping ingredients and sprinkle on top of kugel.

Bake uncovered at 350 degrees for 45 to 60 minutes.

Eva (Brafman) Gross

Eva was born in 1890 in Poland, immigrating as a young girl to Baltimore with her parents, Harris and Rosa. She married Harry Gross and moved to Akron in 1928 with their three children: Estelle, Victor and Mildred. Eva and Harry lived in Akron until 1942, when they moved to Florida, and Eva returned to Baltimore after Harry died in the early 1950s. Granddaughter

Harriet remembers that Eva came to Akron each summer for six weeks, spending her time cooking and watching her favorite television programs, *The Ed Sullivan Show* and *The Lawrence Welk Show*. Harriet recalls her grandmother's traditional Jewish dishes, including bagels, helzel, mandelbrot, noodles and cabbage and gedempte chicken. Eva's challah French toast was loved by all and is still made by her family. Harriet made it as a special treat for her mother, Mildred Stern, when she was in a nursing facility during the COVID-19 lockdown. Mildred was also a wonderful cook and gracious hostess. During their loving marriage of almost sixty-six years, she and her husband, Ludwig, hosted many dinner parties and were members of a gourmet club that researched and created menus of foreign cuisines. Harriet credits Eva and Mildred for imparting a love of cooking, good food and tradition to their children, grandchildren and now great-grandchildren. *Submitted by Eva's granddaughters and grandson Harriet Stern Weinglass, Betsy Kelly and Rob Stern.*

Grandma's Challah French Toast

1 loaf challah (or what's left from Friday night)
8 tablespoons salted or unsalted butter, softened to room temperature
6 large eggs
Dash of salt
Milk
Sugar

Slice challah into ¾-inch slices. Spread one side of each slice generously with butter and poke the other side with a fork to aid in absorbing the egg mixture.

Beat the eggs, salt and splash of milk until combined. Place the bread buttered side up in the egg mixture and allow to become saturated— several minutes or overnight in the refrigerator. Thoroughly grease a cookie sheet and place the bread on the sheet, buttered side up. Sprinkle enough granulated sugar to cover the butter completely.

Bake at 350 degrees for 1 hour, or until the sugar has melted and the tops are golden brown and crispy. Let cool on the pan and serve warm or at room temperature. Leftovers may be stored covered and reheated in oven.

Catherine "Kitty" (Mirman) Miller

Kitty was the daughter of Jacob and Sarah (Kodish) Mirman, emigrants from Vilna, Russia, who followed family who had immigrated to Akron a few years earlier. Jacob came in 1900, followed a year later by Sarah and their one-year-old daughter, Mary, the first of their nine children. Jacob worked as an iron scrap dealer for a few years before establishing himself in the real estate business. He and his brothers—Abraham, Carl and Simon—founded the New Hebrew Congregation in 1905 following a controversial split with the Sons of Peace synagogue on Bowery Street. Kitty grew up on Edgewood Avenue in the heart of Akron's Jewish neighborhood and graduated from West High School in 1925. In 1936, she married Nathan Miller and moved to Cleveland, where they settled and raised their daughters, Hermine and Phyllis. According to Hermine, who still has her mother's recipe box, there was often "a big pile" of cookies waiting for them after school and always challah for Shabbat. Hamantaschen, a traditional Purim treat, is one of Hermine's specialties. Before retiring from her position as activities director for Jewish Senior Housing in Cleveland, she made ten pounds of dough for each building to be divided among the residents, who took shaped hamantaschen back to their apartments to bake. Today, Hermine makes hundreds at a time, delivering or mailing them to grateful family and friends. *Contributed by Kitty's daughter Hermine (Miller) Wieder.*

Hamantaschen

1 cup canola oil
1 ¼ cups sugar
4 eggs
1 teaspoon vanilla extract
2 teaspoons baking powder
½ teaspoon salt
4 to 5 cups flour

Pastry filling: Your choice of pastry filling in a tube or Solo brand filling. Do not use jelly or pie filling.

Mix all ingredients in a large bowl, adding eggs one at a time. Start with 4 cups of flour, adding more until the dough feels like velvet. Set it aside until ready to roll, fill and bake.

Roll dough on floured board or counter until dough is about ¼ inch thick. Cut circles with a round cookie cutter. The remaining dough may be rolled out again to cut additional circles. Place ½ teaspoon of filling in the center and pinch corners to form a triangle. Place on parchment-lined baking sheet.

Bake at 350 degrees for 15 minutes or until evenly browned. Cool on baking rack. Set on a platter to "dry" and crisp. They will become soft if stored in a container.

Helen (Weinberger) Borchardt Davis

After the 1965 death of her mother, Rose (Borchardt) Kahan, Nancy Mermelstein found a recipe card titled "Carrot Cake—Helen's" in her mother's recipe box. Helen was Rose's sister-in-law, the wife of Rose's brother, Gerson Borchardt. Helen was born in Akron in 1915 to Frieda (Klein) and Max Weinberger, who emigrated from Hungary just two years earlier. Helen met Gerson while visiting his hometown of Chicago, and they married in Akron in 1943 while Gerson was serving in the air force. After the war, they remained in Akron, where they raised their daughter and Gerson was a successful real estate broker. After Gerson died in 1983, Helen married Harry Davis. She was a member of Anshe Sfard, Beth El Sisterhood, the Jewish Center, B'nai B'rith and Hadassah. Nancy's marriage to Mel Mermelstein is the product of a shidduch (Yiddish for match) arranged by her aunt Helen and uncle Gerson and Mel's parents, Julia and Martin Mermelstein, who knew Helen's father, Max, in the old country. Nancy recalls fondly the many Jewish holidays shared with her aunt and uncle and especially Helen's carrot cake, which was a favorite dessert. Because it doesn't include dairy products, it was parve and could be served after a meat meal. Warm memories of her mother and aunt and uncle are brought back each time Nancy makes this cake. *Submitted by Helen's niece Nancy (Kahan) Mermelstein.*

Carrot Cake

1 ½ cups vegetable oil
2 cups sugar
4 eggs, beaten
3 cups flour

2 teaspoons baking powder
2 teaspoons baking soda
2 teaspoons cinnamon
1 teaspoon salt
2 cups grated carrots
1 cup chopped walnuts

Thoroughly beat oil, sugar and eggs in a large bowl. Add dry ingredients, alternating the nuts and carrots. Mix well. Pour into a well-greased tube or bundt pan.

Bake at 350 degrees for 1 hour and 15 minutes, checking at 55 minutes. Cake is done when tester comes out clean. Remove from oven and cool. Invert onto plate when pan is slightly warm to the touch.

POLISH

When Antone Torowski died in 1936, the *Akron Beacon Journal* reported that he was the oldest Polish resident of the city, having arrived in Akron sometime around 1891. Although we don't know the reason Antone left Poland or why he settled in Akron, he left a country that had suffered political upheaval, border changes and foreign occupation for more than a century. From the 1880s through the early 1900s, millions of Poles left the land of their birth for the United States, making their way to industrial cities like Akron, where most worked as laborers and in factories.

WHERE THEY LIVED

By 1920, more than 1,500 Akron citizens claimed Poland as their place of birth, with twice that number reporting Polish parentage. Following World War II, another wave of Poles made its way to Akron. Like most new immigrants, they settled in neighborhoods among family and friends who had arrived before them. Many of Akron's early Poles found their home in the area just north of downtown, on and around Glenwood Avenue, Canal, Lods, North Howard and North Streets.

Church Life

Church life was especially important to Akron's Polish immigrants. Although some were Jewish, the majority were Roman Catholic. Akron's earliest Catholic Poles attended St. John the Baptist on Brown Street, a church established in 1907 by the Diocese of Cleveland to serve the Slovak and Polish communities of Akron. Some attended St. Vincent Catholic Church, which offered Mass in Polish. In 1912, St. Hedwig's was established as Akron's first Polish church when the diocese sent Father Bronislaw Salomon to start a Polish congregation. That same year, the congregation bought property on Flowers Court in North Hill and began an ambitious building campaign to construct their own house of worship. The modest church, built entirely with money raised by parishioners, was dedicated in 1915. The *Akron Beacon Journal* reported that the membership consisted of "300 families and 200 unmarried people....Among them are a number of Italian families." This building served Akron's Polish Catholics until 1925, when a new building was constructed under the leadership of Father Frank Kozlowski. The first Mass at the new church on Glenwood Avenue was celebrated on Christmas

The 1930 graduating class of St. Hedwig's Church, the first spiritual home of Akron's Polish Catholic community. *Akron–Summit County Public Library.*

Eve in 1925. St. Hedwig's served the spiritual needs of its congregation until 2009, when the diocese ordered its closure due to declining membership and dwindling financial resources. St. Hedwig's offered Mass in Polish until the week before it shuttered its doors.

CLUBS AND ORGANIZATIONS

Social and fraternal clubs were, and still are, important to Akron's Polish community. Among the earliest was the Polish National Alliance, which had three Akron chapters; the Alliance of Poles of America; and two branches of the Polish Roman Catholic Union. Other groups included the Polish Women's Sewing Circle, United Polish Singers, Akron Choir Echo, United Polish American Council, Polish Democratic Club and Polish Federated Merchants. While some were focused mostly on serving as places to gather and celebrate their heritage, others were political, working to help Poles in the old country who were living under oppressive regimes. When World War I broke out, Akron's chapter held patriotic celebrations, flag dedications and fundraisers for a Polish War Work Fund. The national chapter pledged $20 million for this effort, with the Akron chapter asking each Polish family to donate $60 per year. Between World War I and World War II, the Pulaski Post No. 32 of the Polish Legion of American Veterans was established. Named for American Revolution hero Casimir Pulaski, Akron's Polish VFW chapter remains active today at its home on Dayton Street. During World War II, Akron's Poles rallied to help their native county, holding fundraisers to send money overseas. The women of St. Hedwig's Church organized a sewing circle to make clothing for the Red Cross to distribute to children in Poland. After the war, a Polish relief committee consisting of three members from each of the fifteen Polish groups in Summit County and the Polish Volunteers for the American Red Cross went door to door collecting funds for the effort. Their activism did not end with World War II, however. In 1953, the Polish American Political Club hosted a welcoming banquet for fifty displaced persons who came to the United States before a ban was instituted halting the flow of most refugees to this country. In May 1982, members of Akron's Polish community marched, in costume, from Mass at St. Hedwig's to the Polish Legion Veterans Hall in support of Solidarity, the Polish anti-communist movement led by Lech Wałęsa.

The concern and compassion of Akron's Poles for those experiencing oppression extended beyond their people. From the earliest years, they were welcoming and inclusive, even sharing their festivals and buildings with non-Polish groups. In 1916, Akron's Italian and Polish communities came together to celebrate the feast of Maria Santissima del Rosario at the original Polish church at Lods and Flower Streets. In 1923, the Polish Hall on Lods Street was to host a meeting to fight the Ku Klux Klan, which had a firm hold in Akron politics, law enforcement and the school board. In the 1920s and 1930s, the Summit County Colored Democratic Club and the Colored Citizens of Akron met regularly at the Polish Hall. It wasn't all about politics and religion, however. In 1930, Akron's Polish community hosted more than two hundred delegates of the United Polish Singers of America for its annual convention, which commenced with, according to the *Akron Beacon Journal*, a grand concert of "quaint and beautiful folk songs of their native land."

For decades, Akron's Polish clubs celebrated their heritage at their annual picnics, often at Falcon Lake and later at the Ohio Sportsmen Club in Copley. Festivities always included traditional dancing and singing, food, field games and other contests. In August 1949, the Polish Legion of American Veterans featured Stanisław Radwan, a former prisoner of war and contender for the title of "World's Strongest Man." Sometime in the 1970s, Akron's Polish clubs formed an umbrella group, United Polish-American Council of Summit County, under which all of the groups held one picnic and an annual debutante ball.

Today, the Polish American Citizens Club on East Glenwood is the hub of activity for Akron's citizens of Polish heritage. Although some groups were formed before the PACC's founding, it is the longest-existing group, established in 1921. According to the club's written history, it was formed to oversee the trusteeship of the big three: the Polish National Alliance, the Polish Roman Catholic Union and the Alliance of Poles. For two years, club members met at the Polish Hall at 277 North Howard Street, but they soon outgrew that space and moved to the building St. Hedwig's had occupied until the new church was built on East Glenwood. As membership grew, plans were made to construct a new building for the thriving club, and in 1945, they purchased twelve acres on East Glenwood owned by Stephen Kraszewski, a prominent member of Akron's Polish community. In June 1949, the new club was opened. Additions and improvements made in 1958 and 1968 allowed the group to expand its ability to host fundraising events and to offer hall rentals for weddings and other celebrations.

Golabki making is a group effort for members of Akron's Polish American Citizens Club, who make scores of Polish stuffed cabbage for festivals, club dinners and catered events. *Polish American Citizens Club of Akron.*

Food and celebrations are still a focus of the club. On Friday nights, the club fills with hungry diners who come to enjoy perch dinners. In addition to their traditional fried version, beer-battered fish made with Polish beer is offered on the fourth Friday of each month. Other Polish specialties are available throughout the year, including pierogies and golabki (stuffed cabbage). The menu expands for the fall Polish Festival, which features dancing, music, Polish beers and more. Former club kitchen manager Mary Beth Grether has worked hard to preserve and resurrect Polish food traditions at the club. For Easter 2018, the club sold molded butter in the shape of a lamb. When Polish families took their basket of Easter dinner to church to be blessed, it often included a butter lamb, which represents the Lamb of God.

RESTAURANTS AND FOOD BUSINESSES

There was no shortage of neighborhood grocery stores for Akron's Polish Americans. Kwiecinski, Mikolajczk, Pikoski, Sobczak, Suscinski and Wojno are some of the store owner names listed in the 1937 *Akron City Directory*, and almost all were located on or near Glenwood Avenue. One of the earliest and longest-existing was Pikoski Brothers, located first on East North and later on Glenwood, where it was in business for more than fifty years until closing in the early 1960s. Another prominent Polish business owner was Stanley Wozniak, who owned a Square Deal grocery store in South Akron in the 1920s and 1930s. According to his 1937 obituary, although he arrived penniless in 1903, he was able to send his four children to college, including sons Steve and Joe, who became well-known Akron lawyers. It was said that Steve was the first Polish lawyer in the city.

Polish immigrant Joseph Olesky founded the Olesky Meat Packing Company in 1932. Bread and baked goods were offered by several Polish bakeries. One of the earliest was the East North Street Bakery owned by a partnership of several Poles, some of whom formed the Cuyahoga Baking Company in 1920. When it closed in the mid-1950s, the partners were Walter Nivins, Ben Modzeleski and Vincent Kolodziejcak. In 1918, the Akron Rye Bread Company was started by brothers John and Frank Rozewicz. After John died in 1925, it was taken over by August Chrzanowski, Marjan Ogonowski and Vincent Nalencz. Known for its delicious rye and pumpernickel, the bakery was still delivering by horse as late as 1938. An *Akron Beacon Journal* classified advertisement that year announced that the company was "changing to trucks—horses for sale." Frank Rozewicz stayed

Employees and family of the Akron Rye Bread Company established in 1918 by John and Frank Rozewicz. *Pat Groetz Easterwood.*

Advertisement for the International Cafe owned by Polish immigrants Pete and Mary Lepkowski and later their sons Stanley and Walter. Eddie (Edwin) Jarzenski and his band were favorites. *From the Akron Beacon Journal.*

on with the bakery as production manager until 1945, when he and his son, Chester, took over the Kenmore Baking Company.

A number of local watering holes were run by Polish Americans. Among the earliest were multiple establishments operated by Walter Markowski, who arrived from Poland in 1902. By 1912, he was running a saloon on North Howard Street, which was described in old city directories as a "soft drink" business. He later ran the White Eagle Hotel and Cafe on North Main Street. Leonard Kubalak expanded a small sandwich shop on East Tallmadge Avenue to Leon's Tavern and later Leon's Restaurant, which hosted scores of banquets and celebrations in its swanky Bird and Beef Room. In the 1950s, Lawrence and Rosalia Wrobel ran the Lawrence Cafe in the downstairs level of their home on Thornton Street. The International Cafe on Brown Street owned by Pete and Mary Lepkowski featured polka music by regulars Eddie "Tonsils" Jarzenski & His Serenaders, and Zygmunt "Sam" Niewiadomski welcomed guests at his Maple Valley Tavern on Copley Road. In the 1960s and 1970s, the Pogo Drive-In on Canton Road owned by Victor Pogorzelski was a popular hangout for teens.

Akron's Polish community remains strong and tightly connected. Families still celebrate their beloved family traditions, foods and music with the Polish American Club as their hub. As the club's website proclaims, the club "provides a link to our heritage, as well as a communal bridge to our future… remaining for us a comfortable anchor in a world that is ever-changing."

Smacznego!

Polish American Citizens Club of Akron

Everyone has a role in the kitchen when members of the Polish American Citizens Club get together to make pierogi. The assembly line includes mixers, kneaders, rollers, fillers and pinchers. Until a few years ago when the club purchased a special roller, everything was done by hand. These savory and delicious filled dumplings have been made and served for decades at club events, weddings and for the club's weekly Friday fish fry dinners, where they may also be bought frozen by the dozen. According to longtime pierogi maker volunteer Phyllis (Gmerek) Early, the original recipe likely came from Polish-born club members Marianna Wyszynski or Aleksandra Wojcik. Former kitchen manager Mary Beth (Dombrosky) Grether reduced the quantities and adapted it for the home kitchen.

Pierogi

Dough
1 whole egg and 1 yolk, beaten
1 ½ tablespoons vegetable oil
5 cups flour
½ teaspoon salt
1 ⅓ cups warm water

Mix eggs and oil. Mix flour and salt in a large bowl. Create a well in the center of the flour and salt mixture. Pour egg mixture and warm water into the well. Gently mix in flour until liquids are absorbed. Knead by hand until well blended. Cover and let sit for 15 to 20 minutes.

Roll chilled filling into 1-inch balls. As you make the balls, keep the dough covered to prevent it from drying out. On a lightly floured surface, roll out the dough until ⅛ inch thick, but not too thin or it will tear. Dip the edge of a 3-inch diameter glass, cookie cutter or pierogi cutter in flour and cut rounds out of the dough. Dampen the dough edges with water to secure a good seal. Place the prepared filling in the center and fold over the dough to form a half-moon. Pinch edges together to seal.

Place pierogi in boiling salted water until they float and are tender, about 3 to 5 minutes. Remove from water with a slotted spoon and let drain. These are ready to serve, but are better when fried in butter until lightly browned and served with fried onions and sour cream. Pierogi can be frozen after boiling. Arrange on a baking sheet, cover with plastic wrap and place in freezer. Once they are frozen, place them in freezer bags.

Potato Cheese Filling
1 ¼ cups onions, chopped
Bacon drippings from ¼ pound bacon
2 ½ pounds baking potatoes
6 tablespoons butter
¾ to 1 cup cheese—a mixture of sharp and mild Cheddar works well

Cook onion in bacon drippings until translucent. Set aside. Peel potatoes and cut into 1-inch cubes. Cook in salted boiling water until soft. Do not overcook—overcooking will cause the potatoes to become starchy and pasty. Drain potatoes. With mixer or masher, mash potatoes until chunks are broken up. Add butter, cheese and onions. Mix well to remove all lumps. Let cool. When cool, cover and place in the refrigerator overnight.

Sweet Potato Filling
2 ½ pounds sweet potatoes
8 tablespoons unsalted butter, divided
Salt to taste
20 fresh sage leaves, sliced

Peel and cut sweet potatoes into 1-inch pieces. Place in a large pot of water. Bring to a boil until the sweet potatoes are tender when pierced with a fork. Drain and mash with butter and salt. Add sage leaves. Allow to cool.

The Olesky Family

Joseph (Oleszczuk) Olesky was a teenager in 1913 when he emigrated from Pulawy, Poland, to Akron. By 1920, he was married to his first wife, Aniela; had four children; and was working as a baker. Sadly, Aniela died of tuberculosis in 1926, leaving Joseph with their young children. In 1928, he married Anna Piza, the daughter of Polish immigrants, and had three more children. While working hard as a baker during the day, he made sausage in his home at night, peddling it to his fellow North Hill Poles. Joseph's homegrown business was the genesis of the Olesky Packing Company. In 1932, he moved his family to Tallmadge and started his business in a five-car garage where he and his sons Anthony, Walter and Joseph Jr. made and sold quality sausage and pork products for more than thirty years. Joseph and Anna's grandson Stan has warm memories of growing up in Tallmadge near his grandparents, uncles, aunts and cousins, most of whom lived on the same street, as well as almost daily visits to the packing company, which he described as "my playground." Stan makes kielbasa every year for Christmas and Easter, and although he describes his family as mostly Americanized these days, their holiday table always includes this traditional Polish sausage, as well as pierogi and other Polish dishes. Stan's family preserves the Christmas Eve tradition of breaking and sharing oplatki, or Christmas wafers, a Polish tradition observed by Poles for centuries. For years, Stan's grandmother received wafers from her family in Poland. As Stan recalled, "It was a nice way to break bread with them across the ocean." *Contributed by Joseph's grandson Stan Olesky.*

Biala Kielbasa (White Kielbasa)

Recipe note: According to Stan, the seasonings may be adjusted to your taste.

> 10 pounds pork butt, cut up
> 4 tablespoons salt
> 1 tablespoon sugar
> 2 large cloves garlic, minced
> 1 tablespoon coarsely ground black pepper
> 2 teaspoons marjoram
> 2 cups ice water

Grind pork through a ¼-inch or ⅜-inch grinder plate. Add all ingredients and mix until spices are evenly distributed. Stuff into 35- to 38-millimeter hog casings. To cook, simmer in 180-degree water for 15 minutes.

Mary (Dworakowski) Pogorzelski

Sundays were special for Lunora Sadon when she was a girl. Her family always attended noon Mass at St. Hedwig's, followed by a jaunt up the street for drinks at the Polish American Citizens Club, ending at the Glenwood Avenue home of her Babcia (grandmother) and Dziakek (grandfather) Mary and Frank Pogorzelski. The main course was always baked chicken, freshly caught and dressed from their backyard coop. Mary was a young woman in 1902 when she and her sister, Clementine, left Poland for Akron. Frank, from Roszki Ziemaki, Poland, arrived a year later. They were married in 1904 at St. Vincent Church and raised nine children in their North Akron home. Frank worked for International Harvester, Loewenthal Rubber, the Erie Railroad and, finally, Akron Selle Company, from which he retired in 1951. Frank and Mary were charter members of St. Hedwig's, where Frank was the official bell ringer for years, pealing the church bells for weddings, funerals and each day at 6:00 a.m., noon and 6:00 p.m. They were also active members of the Polish Roman Catholic Union, the Polish National Alliance and the Polish American Citizens Club. Granddaughter and family historian Lunora has kept the family connection to the club, managing the kitchen for more than a dozen years and now serving as part of the hardworking pierogi-making team. This recipe for golabki, a staple of Polish family homes, has been passed down through several generations of her family. *Contributed by Lunora (Pogorzelski) Sadon.*

Golabki

1 head cabbage
1 onion, finely chopped
2 tablespoons margarine
1 pound ground beef
½ pound ground pork
2 cups cooked rice
2 eggs
Salt and pepper
1 (14½-ounce) can tomato sauce
1 (14½-ounce) can whole tomatoes

Remove the core from the cabbage. Scald cabbage in boiling water and remove leaves as they soften.

Lightly sauté onions in margarine. Do not let them brown. Combine with beef, pork, rice, eggs and seasonings. Mix well.

Place 2 tablespoons of mixture (more if it is a large cabbage leaf) in the center of each cabbage leaf and roll. Layer rolls in a heavy pan. Pour tomato sauce over rolls, then squeeze tomatoes from the can and arrange on top. Cover and simmer over low heat for 2 hours. Serves 6–8.

The Dombrosky Family

Three Dombrosky siblings made their way to Akron from Pittsburgh, where their Polish/Irish American family had lived since their great-grandparents John and Adamina Dombrosky arrived around the turn of the twentieth century. Dave came first, followed by his brother, John, and sister, Mary Beth. John joined the St. Brendan chapter of the Hibernians Club and the Polish American Citizens Club, soon to be joined by his siblings and Dave's wife, Jeanne Habas, who also has Polish roots. All four are active members of the Polish American Citizens Club. Former kitchen manager Mary Beth organized a successful Polish murder mystery night (the weapon was a bag of frozen pierogi), and she and brother John were planning co-chairs for the club's 2021 centennial. According to Mary Beth, haluski "is a staple at our Polish reunions and family gatherings, even the Irish ones. To me, it is way better than the Polish pickled eggs my dad loved. I thought I might grow to like them. But I still say, 'Give me haluski or give me death, anything but pickled eggs.'" *Contributed by Dave and John Dombrosky and Mary Beth (Dombrosky) Grether.*

Haluski

¾ pound butter
1 medium to large head cabbage, chopped
3 to 4 onions, chopped
1 pound extra-wide egg noodles
Salt and ground black pepper to taste
Optional: To make this a meal, add sliced kielbasa.

Melt butter in a large skillet or heavy pot. Add cabbage and cook for 5 minutes. Add onions and sauté until the cabbage is tender, about 5 to 10 minutes. Cook noodles according to package directions and drain. Sprinkle with a little melted butter or oil and mix to prevent them from sticking. Combine noodles, cabbage, butter and onions and mix well. Add salt and pepper to taste.

Marianna Wyszynski

Marianna immigrated to Canton from Lublin, Poland, in 1960 with her first husband, Walter Zielinski. She was a member of the Polish Women's Alliance, and both were active in the Polish National Alliance (PNA) and All Saints Church in Canton. They attended joint meetings with the Akron branch of the PNA, and that is where Marianna met Tomasz "Tommy" Wyszynski, whom she later married after Walter passed away. Marianna and Tommy were active members of the Polish American Citizens Club of Akron and St. Hedwig's Church. Marianna perfected her kapusta recipe after adding and subtracting ingredients to make it just right. Thousands of helpings of Marianna's kapusta have been served over the years at various club and church events.

Kapusta

1 small head cabbage, sliced
3 onions, chopped
1 pound bacon, ground in grinder or food processor
3 pounds sauerkraut, drained
1 teaspoon salt
1 teaspoon pepper
1 or 2 bay leaves

Boil cabbage for about 10 minutes. Drain and set aside. Sauté onions and bacon in a large skillet or pot until onions are tender. Add cabbage, sauerkraut, salt and pepper and bay leaves.

Place in a covered baking dish and bake at 350 degrees for 2 hours.

Barbara (Cieplechowicz) Niewiadomski

Barbara emigrated from Lublin, Poland, to Akron in 1920. Soon after arriving, she met fellow Pole Zygmunt Niewiadomski at a Polish dance. They were married in 1922 at the original wood frame St. Hedwig's under the old Viaduct bridge. Zygmunt, of Paprotnia, Poland, arrived a few years earlier, having made his way from Buffalo after learning of the plentiful jobs in Akron's booming rubber industry. When World War I broke out, he enlisted in the U.S. Army and served on the European front, receiving a Purple Heart for his service and his American citizenship, of which he was very proud. After returning from the war, he took a job with Firestone, where he worked for twenty-seven years as a tire builder and was credited for devising a method of releasing whitewall tires from molds without marring the white paint. Inspired by watching Barbara use flour to keep her pastry from sticking to the table, he took talc from home and shook it into the tire molds, releasing perfect whitewalls. Like many immigrants, they experienced discrimination at times. While attending a church picnic at Summit Lake, they were approached by a group of Ku Klux Klansmen who told them to leave. Zygmunt responded that he was an American and belonged there. Following a tussle, which the priest tried to break up, Zygmunt turned to him, said, "Forgive me, Father," pushed him aside and promptly knocked out two of the KKK members. The rest of the group made a hasty retreat. Barbara and Zygmunt raised their three children on Julien Avenue in the heart of Akron's Polish neighborhood and were active members of St. Hedwig's as well as several Polish clubs. In 1932, Zygmunt mortgaged the family home to fund and organize the Pulaski Post 32 of the Polish Legion of American Veterans. In 1951, Zygmunt and Barbara opened the Maple Valley Tavern, a popular neighborhood bar, which Zygmunt ran with his son-in-law, Bob Labate, husband of their daughter, Jean. According to Jean, Barbara had a keen mind for business, and Zygmunt and she were true partners in marriage and at work. Bob and Jean went on to open West Akron's beloved Amber Pub in 1968, a favorite restaurant and watering hole of businesspeople and politicians. Known unofficially as the Portage Country Club annex, they ran it until 1996. Jean has fond memories of her mother's cooking, especially her extra-large pierogi and galobki. Jean learned to cook at the heels of her mother, who never wrote her recipes down. The cucumber salad was served as a favorite at the Amber Pub, and according to Jean, it is "very Polish." *Contributed by Barbara's daughter, Jean (Niewiadomski) Labate.*

Cucumber Salad

6 to 8 pickling cucumbers (small ones that come in a package), thinly sliced
Good apple cider vinegar
3 to 4 scallions, sliced (all of the white and some of the green)
2 tablespoons chopped fresh dill or 2 teaspoons dried dill
2 heaping tablespoons sour cream
Salt and pepper

Place cucumbers in a bowl. Add enough vinegar to coat cucumbers. Mix them around a bit and then immediately drain thoroughly. Mix in scallions and dill. Add sour cream, just enough to coat the cucumbers, adding more if desired. Salt and pepper to taste. May be served immediately or refrigerated and served later.

Helen (Lazarski) Gmerek Nahorecki

Helen was just a toddler when her parents, Leon and Josephine Lazarski, made the decision in 1912 to immigrate to America from Warsaw. Her grandmother wouldn't hear of taking such a young child to a new country and insisted that Helen be left with her until Leon and Josephine were settled. Due to World War I, it wasn't until 1924 that Leon was able to return and get Helen, who was by then thirteen years old. When Helen arrived, she met her eight-year-old American-born sister who didn't speak Polish. Until Helen learned English, the sisters communicated with sign language. Leon was a carpenter and used his skills to build a large family home on Julien Avenue, which is still in the family. It is currently owned by Leon's grandson Ray Gmerek, who makes wine from the grapes Leon planted a century ago. According to Leon's granddaughter Phyllis Early, the house includes secret compartments built by Leon to hide his liquor during Prohibition. Helen grew up and lived in that house until she met and married fellow Pole Sylvester Gmerek, who came to Akron by way of Pennsylvania, where he and his brothers worked as coal miners until making their way to Akron for better-paying jobs in the rubber industry. After Sylvester died, she married Michael Nahorecki, also a Polish immigrant. Helen's recipe for babka is an annual Easter tradition among her family, who get together on Good Friday to make twenty to thirty loaves of different shapes and sizes. *Contributed by Helen's daughter Phyllis (Gmerek) Early.*

Babka (Polish Easter Bread)

2 cakes yeast
1 ½ cups sugar, plus an additional tablespoon
1 quart milk, scalded and cooled to lukewarm
9 cups flour
1 tablespoon salt
11 egg yolks
1 teaspoon vanilla
½ pound butter, melted
1 teaspoon grated orange peel
3 to 4 tablespoons seedless or golden raisins (optional)

Crumb Topping
1 cup flour
½ cup sugar
¼ cup melted butter

Topping: Mix flour, sugar and melted butter until it forms into small crumbs, adding more flour if it is too wet or more butter if it is too dry.

Bread: Crumble yeast and 1 tablespoon of sugar into 1 cup of the milk. Set aside until risen and bubbly. Sift flour and salt into a large mixing bowl. In a separate bowl, beat together remaining sugar, 10 egg yolks and vanilla until light, about 20 minutes. Make a well in the center of the flour mixture. Pour in yeast mixture, followed by egg yolk mixture and remaining milk. Mix well. Add melted butter, orange peel and raisins, if desired. Knead until smooth. Cover and let rise until doubled, about 2 hours. Punch down, divide and place in greased loaf pans, filling them about halfway. Cover and let the dough rise to the top of the pans.

Brush with remaining egg yolk and top with crumb mixture.

Bake at 325 degrees for 1 hour or until done. Makes 3 to 4 loaves.

Stan Najeway

Stan was born in 1925 in New Kensington, Pennsylvania, to Polish immigrants, Francis and Frances (Materniak) Najewicz. Francis worked in mining, a major industry in that part of Pennsylvania, home to many eastern

European immigrants. After graduating from high school, he served in the Merchant Marine as a cadet and deck engineer, later attending Wake Forest College, where he was a star basketball player. After graduating in 1951, Stan made his way to Akron for a job as an aviation field representative for Goodyear, where he shared his basketball skills as a forward with the Goodyear Wingfoots. Single at the time, he rented a room on West Market Street from Lucile Orcutt, widow of Akron Paint and Varnish executive Norman Orcutt. In 1955, he married Akronite Patricia Long, a graduate of Our Lady of the Elms and Kent State University. They were blessed with five children. Stan's daughter Anne (Najeway) Vainer has a handwritten Christmas letter from Stan's sister Cecilia (Najewicz) Walsh, written to his wife and Anne's mother, Pat, that includes instructions for making kolaczki, a recipe that has been handed down through four generations of the Najeway family. "Kolaczki are made especially for Christmas, Easter, weddings and funerals. I have memories of my dad's oldest sister making them and, of course, my dad. Love Knots, pierogies, cabbage and noodles and these cookies are the Polish foods we have all grown up on and still make and eat today." *Contributed by Stan's daughter Anne (Najeway) Vainer.*

Kolaczki

Filling
1 pound ground walnuts
¾ cup sugar
6 egg whites, beaten but not stiff
Grated rind of 1 lemon (optional)

Mix ingredients together just before you are ready to roll the cookies.

Dough
1 (2-ounce) cake yeast or 3 packages dry yeast
2 tablespoons sugar
1 pound vegetable shortening
6 egg yolks
1 (12-ounce) can evaporated milk
6 cups flour
1 teaspoon salt
2 tablespoons confectioners' sugar

Dissolve yeast and sugar in ¼ cup lukewarm water until it foams. Mix shortening and egg yolks until well blended. Stir in yeast mixture. Alternately, add the milk, flour and salt. Cover bowl with waxed paper and place in refrigerator for 6 hours or overnight.

Sprinkle a bit of flour and granulated sugar on counter or breadboard. Using one-third of the dough at a time, roll to ⅛-inch thickness and cut into 2-inch squares. Place a teaspoon of filling in the middle and bring opposite corners together, slightly overlapping one corner over the other. If you run out of nut filling, use prune (lekvar) or apricot filling.

Place on a cookie sheet and bake at 350 degrees for 12 to 15 minutes. Remove from cookie sheet and sprinkle with confectioners' sugar.

Jean (Wrobel) Rozewicz

For forty-seven years, Jean helped to manage Kenmore Baking, a family business started by her husband Chester's father, Frank Rozewicz. Frank brought his baking skills to Akron by way of Poland and Beaver Falls, Pennsylvania, where he landed after immigrating in 1907. In 1918, he helped to start the Akron Rye Bread Company, and in 1945, he and Chester bought Kenmore Baking located on Manchester Road. Jean, who had a head for numbers, did the books; Chester's sister Genevieve Kovacs helped out, and daughters Pam and Pat drove delivery trucks during their high school and college years. The bakery served many of Akron's biggest restaurants, as well as customers who came to buy their delicious Vienna bread, hard rolls and Polish specialties like cookies and paska (Polish Easter bread). *Akron Beacon Journal* columnist Ken Nichols reported in 1960 that Nick Yanko contracted with the bakery to make buns for the trendy new "submarine" sandwiches that were all the rage on the East Coast. Yanko's version became its famous "Beachcomber." This recipe was a favorite of Kenmore Baking customers and always included on Rozewicz holiday cookie plates. *Contributed by Jean's daughters Pat (Rozewicz) Groetz-Easterwood and Pam (Rozewicz) Haberkost.*

Migdalowe Polksiezyce (Almond Crescent Cookies)

½ cup butter, softened
⅛ teaspoon almond extract
½ cup confectioners' sugar, plus more for dusting cookies

Pinch of salt
¾ cup flour
I cup ground almonds
¼ cup toasted, chopped almonds

Combine butter, extract and sugar. Add salt, flour, ground almonds and chopped almonds. Mix thoroughly. Wrap dough in plastic wrap and chill in refrigerator for 30 minutes.

Shape rounded teaspoons of dough into crescent shapes. Place on baking sheet and bake at 325 degrees for 15 to 20 minutes until just beginning to brown. Cool on baking sheet for 2 minutes. Remove and dust or roll in confectioners' sugar.

SERBIAN

The history of the former Yugoslavia and the path of its immigrants who arrived on our shores is complex and confusing. Centuries of war, land disputes and other factors led to constantly shifting boundaries and displacement of its citizens. Depending on when they arrived, immigrants from that region of Europe declared various countries as their homeland based on their country of allegiance and when they left. The largest group to make Akron home is Serbian. Although members of Akron's community trace their origins to several regions of the former Yugoslavia, they identify as Serbian, unified mostly by their culture and faith rather than the country or region from which they came.

Although Serbs were coming to the United States as early as the 1880s, the earliest in Ohio arrived just before and after the turn of the twentieth century, the majority settling in the Cleveland area, with a few making their way to Akron. The greatest influx of Serbs to Akron arrived after World War I, followed by an additional wave of displaced persons who came after World War II. Decades later, another wave arrived during and following the 1990s war in Bosnia and Herzegovina, Slovenia and Croatia. With the help of the International Institute of Akron, dozens who fled to the United States from countries of the former Yugoslavia came to Akron, bringing with them their skills and drive to make a better life. United Nations statistics show that immigrants from this region consistently rank highest among other refugee groups for rates of homeownership, level of education, business ownership and labor participation.

Where They Lived

Many of Akron's early arrivals settled on the east side of town around Case Avenue. Kochoff, Kovacic, Vujanov, Petkanich and Mulatich are some of the Serbian names listed on Case Avenue in the 1920 *Akron City Directory*. Other enclaves were located near the Serbian Home on Ira Avenue and later in the vicinity of St. Demetrius Church on Lake Street. Some landed in the German and eastern European neighborhood of Goosetown near Grant Street, and many more made their homes in Barberton. With the assistance of the International Institute of Akron, many of those who arrived following the war of the 1990s settled in North Akron, as well as other areas of the city, often living together in apartment complexes. Today's Serbs live throughout Akron, as well as surrounding communities, especially Barberton.

Church Life

Before establishing a church home of its own, Akron's Serbian community met at the Barberton Serbian Home founded in 1912, St. Mary's Russian Orthodox Church on South Street (now St. Elia the Prophet) and sometimes in private homes. In 1918, a priest was appointed, and property was purchased on Ira Avenue to build a hall where they could meet and worship. Within a year, the new congregation of St. Demetrius had raised enough funds, including pledges of $500 from Firestone, Goodyear and Goodrich, to start construction. On June 13, 1920, they dedicated their new hall, celebrating with a day of events that included local dignitaries as well as the Serbian ambassador to the United States. A classified ad for rental of the hall boasted of "a good big stage for plays, fine big dancing floor, and good lodge room." Although the hall served them well for more than ten years, they longed for a traditional church. Despite the Depression and the economic hardship of its members, the congregation raised enough funds and harnessed the free labor of its members to build a new church. In 1933, a beautiful new sanctuary on Lake Street was dedicated. Constructed in a traditional Byzantine style, it didn't have pews, in keeping with the tradition of standing during church services. According to a church history, "It was a glorious example of faith and perseverance, a well-known trait of our people."

Before Akron's Serbian community had its own home, they met and worshipped at the Barberton Serbian Home. This photo shows a group of Akron Serbs in front of the Barberton home. *St. Demetrius Serbian Orthodox Church.*

St. Demetrius grew and thrived until 1963, when a schism within the Serbian Diocese of North America spread to Akron's church. St. Demetrius split, with nearly half of the parishioners leaving to form a new congregation, St. Demetrius Congregation. They met at a temporary location on South High Street until purchasing a church building on Waterloo Road. In 1973, that congregation changed its name to St. Archangel Michael Serbian Orthodox Church and moved to Pickle Road, where they built a hall large enough for church services and Sunday school. After more than ten years of raising funds through catered events, bazaars and fish fries, the congregation dedicated a modern new sanctuary in 1987. Home to many Serb families who fled their country following the wars of the 1990s, St. Archangel Michael serves as a social center and place where they can preserve and celebrate their culture and language. According to parish priest Father Milan Pajić, more than 90 percent of its parishioners arrived since the 1990s. The church provided great support to these new arrivals, and many members who were business owners offered jobs to the newly arrived. St. Archangel Michael embraces its heritage and instills pride in its children through Sunday school,

Parishioners of St. Demetrius Serbian Orthodox Church pose in front of their new Lake Street church building dedicated in 1933. *St. Demetrius Serbian Orthodox Church.*

where they are taught Serbian history, language and culture, and its active Folklore Society, where they learn traditional dance and music. St. Archangel Michael shares its heritage with the community each year during Serb Fest, a summer event featuring traditional foods, music, dancing and tables laden with cookies and pastries for sale.

St. Demetrius remained at the Lake Street location until 1984, when the congregation dedicated a new chapel on Ridgewood Road, where the original Lake Street church's icon screen was preserved and installed. In less than ten years, the mortgage was paid off thanks to the commitment of parishioners and friends. By 1994, they had started to plan for a "proper church," and ground was broken that year. Designed by local church architect and fellow Serb Trefon Sagadencky, their new home on Ridgewood was dedicated two years later. They too welcomed and supported immigrants who arrived following the wars of the 1990s. The members of St. Demetrius Serbian Orthodox Church take great pride in the heritage of their church and its one-hundred-plus-year history of service to Akron's Serbian Orthodox

Left: St. Michael Archangel Serbian Orthodox Church in Springfield Township. *Author's collection.*

Below: The iconostasis of the first St. Demetrius on Lake Street was disassembled and moved to its new church building on Ridgewood Road. *Milorad Jovich.*

community and work to keep it alive through various programs, events and Sunday school, where its young members learn the Serbian language. Its Kolo Sestara group supports the church through social events and fundraising, including dinners, dances and festivals.

Although most Serbs are Eastern Orthodox, some are members of the Apostolic Christian Church, which has its roots in the Anabaptist tradition, known in eastern Europe as Nazarenes, which included people of German, Hungarian, Romanian, Slovak, Croatian and Serbian descent. Among the first congregations were North Akron Apostolic on Avon Street, Serbian Apostolic Christian Church on Inman and Apostolic Christian on Berry Street. The successor of North Akron Apostolic is Lakeside Christian Church in Bath Township. The Apostolic Christian Church of West Akron in Copley Township and Norton Apostolic Christian Church are affiliated with the more conservative Nazarean Division of the Apostolic Christian Church.

SOCIAL CLUBS

Akron's early Serbs established more than a dozen clubs, some social, some political. The first was the Vuk Stefanović Karadžić chapter of the Serbian National Federation, started around 1914. Proud to be Americans, they were anxious to participate in all patriotic events and, in that year, held a special flag dedication for Serbian and American flags, a daylong event that included a parade, ceremony and banquet. The Akron chapter of the Serbian National Defense League was formed four years later in support of Yugoslavia during the Great War. According to the *Akron Beacon Journal*, more than one thousand "southern Slavs" met in January at the GAR Hall on Howard Street to endorse a resolution to be sent to President Wilson "to cheer with the greatest enthusiasm the declaration of war on Austria-Hungary." In 1918, the Serbian National Defense League launched a campaign to raise funds to build a home for more than one hundred Serbian orphans who lost their parents during the war.

Later clubs included the American Serbian Civic Club, four branches of the Serb National Federation, Serbian National Home Association, Yugo-Slav Athletic Club, Serbia Club and the Serbian Athletic Club. Akron's Serbian clubs met at various locations until 1920, when the Serbian Home was built on Ira Avenue. The June 13 dedication included a parade from Ira

Avenue through downtown to the Armory, where the group was welcomed by Mayor Carl Beck.

Serbian women, who formed their own groups, were often the driving force behind events and fundraisers. The first ladies' group was the Serbian Ladies Aid Society, which was formed to raise funds for war widows and orphans during World War I. No longer active, Srpska Zenska Zadruga was founded in 1922 by women of St. Demetrius Serbian Orthodox Church. In 1942, they worked with the Red Cross to knit sweaters for American soldiers on the front. Another group affiliated with the original St. Demetrius was Kolo Srpskih Sestara or Circle of Serbian Sisters, founded in 1934. Today, St. Demetrius and St. Michael Archangel count on their Kolo groups to oversee many of their church fundraisers and festivals.

Picnics were an annual event where these groups joined together to celebrate their heritage. In 1938, more than a dozen Serbian groups co-sponsored their first annual Serbian Day at Roma Park. All celebrations included traditional Serbian food, dancing, singing and often concerts by Akron's nationally famous Isidor Bajich Serbian Choir. Akron's Serbs were also proud of singer and hometown girl Vinka Ellesin. She was known as the Queen of Sevdalinka for her traditional singing style of Yugoslavian folk songs.

RESTAURANTS AND FOOD BUSINESSES

Immigrants from Serbia were well represented among Akron's early food businesses. Panto Zaklan ran his Chittenden grocery store from 1921 until 1956. After her husband, Vasa, died in 1932, Rose Stojanovich continued to operate her family grocery on East Avenue. Stephen Bozin's grocery on West Bartges served that neighborhood until he died in 1955. Nicola Dimoff opened the Balkan Bakery on Upson Street in the early 1920s. It later moved to East South Street and then in 1961 to its final location on Manchester Road under the ownership of James Mahailovich. Cheda's Bakery was an Akron favorite. Cheda Kostantinovich opened his business in 1915 in a house on Getz Street, moving to Miami Street, East South and finally to Grant Street. Each morning, he loaded hundreds of loaves of fresh bread on his two-horse wagon for delivery to his customers, always finishing his route by noon. Until closing in 1983, the family-owned bakery was known for its delicious Vienna bread and other fresh baked goods. One of Akron's longest-operating Serb-owned food businesses was Galat Packing Company, founded in 1922 by George Galat. For more than sixty years, Galat's famous Corndale brand of sausage, wieners, bologna and other meat products could be found at Akron grocery stores, and its lard, sold in fifty-pound buckets, was a staple of Barberton's fried chicken joints.

There were plenty of restaurants and taverns, too. A 1919 *Akron Evening Times* advertisement offered Christmas greetings and an invitation to dine at Steve Horvath's Serbian Home Restaurant, Marco Kalenich's American-Serbian Restaurant and the Belmont Hotel run by Kosta Stojakovich. All were located on North Howard Street in Akron's busy commercial district and home to many immigrant-owned restaurants, taverns and confectioneries. Others were located throughout the city, especially near the bustling rubber factories. The popular Brooklands Cafe was run by Stephen Esakov, who started as a grocer. The daughter of a Croatian father and Serbian mother, Sofi (Rauzan) Schmidt opened the Lodge in the former Willow Inn located at the corner of Akron-Peninsula Road and Portage Trail. It was there for twenty years until 1986, when it became

Brothers Glisha, Theodore and Riste Lontchar pose proudly in front of their Ira Avenue grocery. Theodore later owned Bigloaf Bakery on Steiner Avenue. *Phyllis Jovich.*

the home of Papa Joe's. Milo, Mark and Mike Milkovich owned the Olde Loyal Oak Tavern, a cozy fine-dining eatery that operated from 1987 until 2004 in a circa 1845 stagecoach stop on Wadsworth Road.

Keeping eastern European food traditions alive today is the New Era Restaurant, opened in 1937 by Rade and Lucija Juric, who started it to provide quality low-cost meals to the workingman and his family. In 1958, they brought Lucija's cousin Lou Strebick over from Croatia. Now in her nineties, she still works at the restaurant and makes all of their famous strudels by hand. The New Era is now operated by Lou's daughter and her husband Mary and Milos Lekic. Kifli's Bakery and Cafe on State Road is the newest on the scene. Opened in 2001 by Mire and Svjetlana Udovicic, its menu includes traditional Serbian dishes like burek and cevapi. The attached bakery and shop is stocked with eastern European grocery items as well as house-made pastries, including their famous strudel and kifli.

Although not so much an Akron thing, fried chicken lovers make their way to Barberton for Serbian fried chicken, a culinary gift from our Serbian immigrant community. With wit and great detail, former Akronite Ron Koltnow's book *Barberton Fried Chicken, an Ohio Original* offers a fun and fascinating look at the history and culture of Barberton's famous Serbian-style chicken.

Whether they arrived before or after World War I or following the strife of the 1990s, those who made their way to Akron found a welcoming community. Solid, hardworking and patriotic, Akron's Serbs are close-knit and supportive of one another. Regardless of their origin or when they came, their faith, pride and dedication to preserving their heritage will continue to enrich our city.

Prijatno!

Vidosava "Vida" (Vujic) Milovancev

This recipe is presented to honor our mother, Vida, who was born in Voganj in the former Yugoslavia, a small village between Sremska Mitrovica and Ruma. Our father, Branislav (Branko), and Vida immigrated to Akron in July 1968, following family that had previously immigrated to Akron. They came to the United States for religious freedom, to flee communism and to give their children a better life. Vida's first job was with the San Hygiene Upholstery Company, and she later worked from home as a seamstress and bookkeeper for our father's cabinetry and finish carpentry companies.

Only God knows how many generations old this chicken noodle soup recipe is, as it has been passed down from one generation to the next. It is a common meal in the former Yugoslavia, with each family having its own nuanced ingredients and a (usually) highly guarded recipe. We enjoyed this soup as a family almost every Sunday lunch, as well as all holidays and other special occasions. It was commonly served with fried chicken, potatoes and "sausa" (a homemade red sauce). It was also a remedy when one of us was sick—nothing is better for a sore throat! It is a reminder of our family's history and is still made to this day. Vida resides in Bath Township and still sews, cooks and enjoys spending time with her children and grandchildren who all love this soup. Contributed by Vida's son Michael Milovancev.

Sunday Chicken Noodle Soup

1 large white or yellow onion, cut in half
1 whole chicken, washed and cut into pieces
2 teaspoons salt
2 parsley roots
2 parsnip roots
1 celery root
4 carrots
20 stems fresh parsley
2 leeks, washed, dark green leaves cut off, sliced vertically
1 heaping tablespoon Vegeta seasoning (available at some grocery stores and online)
Noodles (homemade or purchased)

Grill onion, cut side down on stovetop over medium-high heat until golden brown. Place chicken in large, deep pot and cover with cold water. Add onion and salt.

Wash and peel roots and carrots, reserving parsley leaves and stems. Cut in half lengthwise and add to pot, along with parsley. Wash leeks, remove root ends and cut off dark green leaves. Cut in half lengthwise and add white and light green stalks to pot.

Cover the pot and bring to a boil on high heat. Once the soup has hard-boiled for a few minutes, reduce heat to medium and simmer for 2 hours. Skim off and discard any fat foam that rises. After 2 hours, add Vegeta, reduce heat to low and simmer for an additional hour. Taste soup and add additional salt or Vegeta to taste.

Strain broth with wire strainer into another large pot. Allow chicken and vegetables to cool in original pot. Broth can be used immediately or refrigerated for later use. To serve immediately, add noodles and cook until done, about 5 to 10 minutes depending on the size of noodles. Pieces of chicken and carrots and other vegetables may be added if desired.

The remaining chicken and vegetables (chopped into ¼-inch dice) may be mixed with mayonnaise, chopped dill pickles, chopped hard-boiled eggs and salt for a delicious chicken salad.

Mary (Okich) Lubyon

Julia Okich was a young widow when she left her home and daughter to immigrate to Akron, joining others from her village of Brod in the Serbian Republic. Her plan was to establish herself before sending for her daughter, Mary, whom she left with family. The day after Julia arrived, Archduke Ferdinand was assassinated, thwarting that plan. It wasn't until 1920 that she could return to Serbia for Mary. In the meantime, Julia had met and married Eli George, who emigrated in 1912 from Tetovo, Serbia, now Macedonia. Eli ran a restaurant on Case Avenue in the 1920s and on Englewood Avenue until retiring in 1941. Mary married Nick Anich, a Croatian immigrant who arrived in Akron in 1919. The two owned a restaurant on Ackley Street in the 1920s, and a family story involves Mary's arrest for bootlegging from their business. A young Wendell Willkie handled her case, and she was acquitted. Mary's recipe for gibanica was passed on to granddaughter and family historian Jane Hull. The original recipe was simply, "You mix up some feta and ricotta with egg. Layer that with filo like you are making baklava. It should be salty." Jane's version is a bit more detailed but results in a traditional Serbian dish that is enjoyed by her family at Christmas and other large gatherings. *Submitted by Mary's granddaughter Jane Hull.*

Gibanica

1 package frozen filo dough, defrosted in refrigerator overnight
1 ½ pounds feta cheese
1 ½ pounds ricotta cheese
Salt
3 eggs
1 ¼ pounds salted butter, melted

Remove filo from refrigerator and allow to come to room temperature, about 2 hours. Slightly dampen two kitchen towels.

Drain and crumble feta, reserving the brine. Mix feta with ricotta and taste for salt. It should be fairly salty. Add salt to taste. Add eggs and mix well. If too dry, add a bit of the reserved brine. Preheat oven to 350 degrees.

Place damp towel on work surface. Open filo and trim to fit a 9 x 13 baking pan. Place filo (on plastic packaging) on top of towel and cover with second towel. Generously butter the bottom of a baking pan and layer 8 sheets of filo, buttering each layer with a pastry brush. Add ¼ of cheese mixture and repeat, ending with filo on the top.

Butter the top and bake at 350 degrees for 1 hour or until golden brown and cheese is set. Let sit for 15 to 20 minutes before cutting into 12 pieces.

Kolo Sestara of St. Demetrius Serbian Orthodox Church

Being a member of St. Demetrius Serbian Orthodox Church for about fifty-two years, I have had the pleasure of observing the Kolo Sestara (Sisters) stretch dough for strudels, make homemade noodles, cabbage rolls, homemade bread and other delicious dishes. In the old days, they prepared the food without recipes and modern appliances like large mixers, fryers, dishwashers. These amazing and hardworking Sisters are involved in the preparation of food for a variety of events including Slavas, weddings, Sunday meals, picnics and other events. From krofne (doughnuts) to cevapi (meat sausages), they make everything with care and attention, giving their time and effort to prepare a variety of meals for families all year long. It is such an honor that the Sisters have chosen me to be president of the community of Kolo Sestara. I am blessed to have a wonderful team of Sisters who continue the traditions that started more than one hundred years ago. This old and favorite recipe from the Kolo Sestara is served at numerous events at St. Demetrius. Many variations can be made to the recipe by adding various amounts of vegetables. Contributed by Milka Vukelic, president, Kolo Sestara of St. Demetrius Serbian Orthodox Church.

Cabbage and Noodles

1 cup vegetable oil
1 pound chopped onions
2 stalks chopped celery
2 large chopped carrots
1 chopped parsnip
2 cloves chopped garlic
1 tablespoon salt
1 large head cabbage, shredded
Salt and pepper
1 pound dried noodles

Heat oil in large skillet. Add onions, celery, carrots, parsnip, garlic and salt. Cover and sauté until tender. Add shredded cabbage. Sauté and simmer until tender. Add water if cabbage mixture becomes dry. Season with salt and pepper.

Boil noodles according to package directions. Drain and add to cabbage mixture and mix well. Season with salt and pepper.

Smiljana (Begecki) Topalsky

My maternal grandmother, Smiljana (Begecki) Topalsky, was born in the village of Nadalj, Serbia. She came to the Akron-Barberton area in 1906 and decided to stay here because there was a well-established Serbian community in the area already at that time. As a young girl, she worked with her mother at the Diamond Match Company that was founded by O.C. Barber. She always had a passion for cooking, and she cooked every day for her family. After she married the love of her life, Manojlo Topalsky, they opened a diner which later became the restaurant Belgrade Gardens, in operation since 1933. Her favorite meal to cook, after fried chicken, was chicken paprikash, a traditional recipe from the region of Serbia that she came from (Vojvodina). This recipe is timeless and I would say more than hundreds of years old. Since paprikash required hours to prepare, it was usually served on Sunday. This recipe has been made at my family restaurant Belgrade Gardens for almost ninety years. Submitted by Smiljana's grandson Milos K. Papich.

Chicken Paprikash

Paprikash
½ cup vegetable oil
2 large onions, chopped
2 stalks celery, sliced
2 carrots, sliced
1 parsley root, sliced
2 Hungarian peppers, sliced into rings (or 1 for less spicy)
1 teaspoon salt
1 teaspoon black pepper
1 tablespoon Vegeta seasoning
2 tablespoons sweet paprika
1 teaspoon crushed red pepper
1 whole chicken, cut up into 8 or 10 pieces
1 to 1½ cups water

Dumplings
3 eggs, beaten
1 teaspoon salt
1 teaspoon baking powder
12 tablespoons flour

Heat the oil in a large pot and sauté onions until tender. Add remaining vegetables and seasonings. Stir well and continue to sauté. Add the chicken and water and simmer for 2 hours. You will know that the paprikash is done when the chicken is almost falling off the bone.

While the paprikash is cooking, make the dumplings. Mix all ingredients well. Bring a pot of salted water to a boil. Drop spoonfuls of dumpling batter into the boiling water. They are done when they rise to the top. Add dumplings to pot with chicken, stirring gently to coat them with the juices.

Gerry (Rogish) Ostich

A first-generation American, Gerry was born in Akron in 1936 to her Croatian mother, Grace (Basich), and Serbian father, Nick Rogish. In 1957, she married George Ostich, the son of Milos and Persa, Serbian immigrants who met and married in Akron in 1924. When George was just twenty-three, he bought and de-constructed an old building in Cleveland and moved it to Wingate Avenue in Akron, where he planned to reconstruct and sell it. At the encouragement of his mother, Persa, he kept the building and two years later started a foundry with skills he learned from his brother-in-law, John Swaino. Now operated by the third generation of Gerry and George's family, Akron Foundry has been designing and creating high-quality aluminum casting for more than seventy years. George and Gerry were active members of St. Michael Archangel Orthodox Church and provided jobs to sixty-two Bosnian church members who came here following the Bosnian War. Gerry was vice-president of the company and served for many years as president of Kolo Srpska Sestara, St. Michael Archangel's ladies' group. She learned many beautiful and delicious recipes from her mother, Grace; mother-in-law, Persa; and her aunt Daša. Gerry is passionate about her church and her family and enjoys teaching the next generation about cooking and Serbian traditions.

Krofne (Serbian Donuts)

½ cup warm milk
1 ounce dry yeast
1 teaspoon flour
2 eggs
3 teaspoons sugar

1 teaspoon salt
8 ounces butter, melted
6 cups flour plus 1 teaspoon for yeast mixture
¾ cup milk
Vegetable oil for frying
Powdered sugar

Mix warm milk, yeast and 1 teaspoon flour in large bowl. Set aside. In another bowl, mix eggs, sugar, salt and butter. Add to yeast mixture. Alternately add the flour and milk and mix until the dough is soft.

Cover dough and place in a warm spot until it has doubled in size. Push dough down and let it rise a second time until doubled.

Remove dough and place on floured board. Roll dough to ½-inch thickness. Cover with a dishtowel for 20 minutes. Use a glass or doughnut cutter to cut round shapes. Using remaining scraps, continue to roll and cut dough.

Heat the oil in a deep frying pan. Fry donuts until golden brown, turning once. Dust with powdered sugar.

Milorad Jovich

Milorad's father, Vladimir, was born in Cincinnati in 1911 to Serbian immigrants, Ignojt and Katica Jovich. When he was just two years old, the young family returned to their Serbian homeland. Following his graduation from a government railroad school in Belgrade, he took a job with the Serbian railroad system, where he worked for thirteen years. When the communist regime of Tito became unbearable, he left. With his American birth certificate in hand, he walked across Serbia, making his way to Hungary, where he was able to board a mail plane bound for the United States. He lived in Buffalo for a short time until moving to Akron, where his first job was pulling weeds for Firestone Tire and Rubber Company. Soon, friends introduced him to Natalie Gradinaz, a young woman who spoke Serbian and was the daughter of Serbian immigrants, Louis and Milica of Barberton. Natalie was able to get Vladimir a job with the Acme grocery where she worked. Their romance bloomed, and the couple was married in 1950 at St. Demetrius Serbian Orthodox Church. Three sons—Milorad, Bozidar and Branko—followed. Vladimir continued to work in the grocery business for many years, and Natalie was active with

St. Demetrius, where she was a member of the Kolo Sestara women's group. Son Milorad serves as president of the congregation and has been deeply involved with the church for decades, becoming the youngest board member at age eighteen. Slava is an important tradition where Serbian families and their friends gather every year to honor their family's patron saint. Milorad's family's patron saint is St. John the Baptist, whose feast day is January 20. Slava bread or Slavski Kolach is served following a ritual symbolic blessing, cutting and offering. Milorad is not certain of the origin of his family recipe but knows that it has been "passed around" for generations. He treasures his collection of more than one hundred recipes handwritten by his mother.

Slavski Kolach

½ cup solid vegetable shortening
2 cups milk
1 teaspoon salt
2 cakes yeast
½ cup sugar
6 to 6½ cups flour
2 eggs, plus 3 egg yolks (sometimes I just use 3 eggs)
½ cup butter, softened

Melt shortening and add milk and salt. This mixture should be warm but not hot. In a separate bowl, stir yeast cakes and sugar together until liquified. Pour into shortening and milk mixture, coating the inner surface of the bowl. Add flour, eggs and 2 egg yolks. Mix thoroughly. Knead by hand or with a dough hook until smooth. Place dough into a lightly greased bowl. Cover with a towel so the top does not get dry. Let it rest until double in size. If it's cold, place it in a warmed oven.

Add butter and continue to mix until smooth. Some recipes call for a second rising before shaping and rising again. I have done both, and it seems to come out the same. Cut the dough in thirds, roll and braid. Let rise until double in bulk. Place in a greased heavy round pan, approximately 10-inch diameter. An ovenproof stew pot or Dutch oven works well.

Bake at 350 degrees for about 1 hour until it pulls from the side of the pan. Make an egg wash with the remaining yolk and 2 tablespoons of water. About 5 minutes before bread is done, use a pastry brush to paint the top of the loaf with the egg wash. Return to oven for the remaining 5 minutes.

Mileva (Milkovic) Rabljenovic

Milka's grandfather Milo Milkovic made his way from the former Yugoslavia to Akron by way of Argentina. After spending time in a German camp following World War II, he was given the option to return home or go someplace else. He chose Argentina, where an uncle was living, but he discovered that it wasn't for him. In 1950, he traveled and joined his uncle Ilija, who was living in Akron. Milka; her parents, Milan and Marija (Milkovic) Vrhovac; and her sisters, Anka and Vesna, left their hometown of Dvor Jovac in 1969 to join members of her mother's (Marija) family in Akron. Milka was fourteen years old when she arrived in America.

Milka credits her mother's sister-in-law, Aunt Milunka "Millie" Milkovic, with teaching her to cook when she was newly married. Her family has belonged to St. Demetrius Serbian Orthodox Church for many years, and she is the president of the church's Kolo Sestara group.

This recipe for Stefani Torta has been in our family for a few generations, as far as I can recall. It was handed down to me by my aunt (mother's sister) Mileva (Milkovic) Rabljenovic. I watched her make and bake this torta when I was a little girl in former Yugoslavia. She had no electricity, running water or modern appliances, but she was a seamstress and a wonderful cook and baker. Can you imagine making a torta without electricity or running water, baking it in a wood-burning stove and beating egg whites with a fork? It took a long time to beat the egg whites with a fork, but she had patience and made wonderful tortas, cookies and meals that tasted delicious. I have been making this torta for over forty years. With modern appliances, it is a bit quicker to make, but Tetka Mileva's torta tasted better to me than mine. Maybe it was that wood-burning stove that made the difference. The recipe was originally written in grams, but I have converted it into cups. I have now given this recipe to my daughter and want to make sure that she passes it on to my granddaughter. Contributed by Milka (Vrhovac) Vukelic.

Stefani Torta

Cake Layer
8 eggs
1 cup sugar
½ cup bread crumbs
1 cup ground walnuts

Filling
4 eggs
¾ cup sugar
3 tablespoons water
¾ cup chocolate chips
1 cup softened butter

Cake: Separate eggs. Beat egg whites until stiff. In a separate bowl, beat egg yolks until fluffy. Add sugar to yolks, mix until fluffy. Fold in bread crumbs and ground walnuts with spatula. Slowly fold in egg whites. Pour batter into 3 greased round cake pans. Bake at 350 degrees for approximately 15 minutes. Do not overbake. Allow to cool completely.

Filling: In a saucepan, beat eggs, sugar and water. Place over medium-low heat. Add chocolate chips, stir and cook until thickened. Remove from heat and cool. Add butter and mix well. Frost cake.

Danica (Tyirin) Velemirov

The daughter of Serbian immigrants, Milutin and Misirka Tyirin, Danica was born in and grew up in Cincinnati. After graduating from the University of Cincinnati, she earned her pilot's license and served in the Civil Air Patrol during World War II. When her beau, Danilo Velemirov, returned from the war—he served in the Pacific with the air force—the two married. An Akron boy, Danilo was the son of Arkadia and Matza Velemirov; his father emigrated from Serbia in 1914, followed later by his mother. After Danica and Danilo's wedding in 1946, they moved to Akron, where they raised their three children: Michael, Danielle and Milana. Danilo worked as a mason and bricklayer, and Danica worked in retail for many years. Both were active members of St. Demetrius and later St. Archangel Michael Serbian Orthodox Churches, where Danica was a member of the Srpska

Zenska Zadruga women's group and served as president of the Isador Bajich Serbian choir. Danilo hosted the *Serbian American Cultural Radio Hour*, which aired on the University of Akron's radio station on Sundays. After his death, daughters Milana and Danielle took it over for a few years. Milana remembers family visits to Cincinnati, where she watched her grandmother Misirka make filo by "throwing everything on a board and mixing it up. She never used recipes." Although Milana didn't pay much attention at the time, she has worked for years to reproduce her mother and grandmother's recipes—"It connects me to my family."

My mom baked many desserts for Christmas and always used the large pastry board and rolling pin made by her father to mix and roll out her dough. My sister Danielle (Velemirov) Otterman now has the board and rolling pin. We have a large gathering at our house every Christmas Eve, and these are two of the desserts that I include in my baking. I will never be a baker equal to my mother, but after twenty-five-plus years I think I do a pretty good job. This recipe makes two kinds of cookies, but you can also make one or the other.

Contributed by Danica's daughter Milana (Velemirov) Estrada.

Gorabia (Serbian Cut-Out Cookies)

Dough
1 pound butter, room temperature
4 cups sifted flour (be sure to sift before measuring)
2 cups sugar
Juice and zest of 1 lemon
6 egg yolks (reserve whites for this recipe and Lazy Cake recipe)
2 tablespoons sour cream

Topping
4 tablespoons ground walnuts
4 tablespoons sugar
3 egg whites

Do this all on the table or pastry board. Using your hands, mix the butter and flour in a circular motion (do not knead). Add sugar and mix. Make a well in the center and add lemon juice, zest, egg yolks and sour cream. Continue mixing by hand to make a soft dough. Generously flour your pastry board or counter and top of the dough. Roll out dough to about ¼ inch. Dip cookie cutters in flour and cut out. Reserve remaining dough to make Lazy Cake (Lenja Pita).

To make topping, combine walnuts and sugar in a small dish. In another small dish take 3 of the egg whites remaining from the gorabia and whip them until mixed thoroughly. Dip cookies in the egg white and then in the sugar nut mixture.

Place on a baking sheet and bake at 350 degrees for 15 to 25 minutes, checking after 15 minutes to see if they are getting done on the bottom. These freeze well.

Lenja Pita (Lazy Cake)

These are made with the dough left after you cut out the gorabia cookies.
Leftover cookie dough
Apricot or plum jelly or preserves
3 egg whites remaining from gorabia
6 heaping tablespoons sugar
6 heaping tablespoons ground walnuts
1 tablespoon vanilla

Place dough on the bottom of a baking sheet with sides, press in place all over (should be about ¼ inch thick). Take a fork and poke all over. Bake in a 350-degree oven for 5 minutes.

Remove and spread generously with jelly or preserves. Place back in oven while you beat egg whites with sugar until stiff. Fold in walnuts and vanilla. Remove dough from oven. Spread egg white and nut mixture over dough. Return to oven and bake until the top gets brown and a little hard—check after about 15 minutes. Remove from oven and cut into squares or 1x2– or 1x3–inch rectangles. Freezes well.

Mary (Smargie) Vukelich

Mary was born in 1910 in Masontown, Pennsylvania, to Serbian immigrants Anna (Dokich) and Peter Smargie (Samardzija), who was employed in southwestern Pennsylvania's coke industry. In 1927, she made her way to Akron, following family members who were living and working here. Mary soon met Mike Vukelich from Denbo, Pennsylvania, also the product of Serbian immigrant parents. After marrying in 1931, the newlyweds lived for a time with Mike's parents, Nick and Mary (Mamula) Vukelich, who lived on Kline Avenue. Mike worked for Goodyear and later owned a trucking business that sold sand and gravel to home construction companies. Mary and Mike were blessed with five daughters. According to daughter Natalie Alexander, "Mother was truly a Serbian woman. She mostly stayed home, took care of the family and cooked meals." Mary and Mike were members of St. Demetrius Serbian Orthodox Church until joining St. Archangel Michael, where Mike was a tutor, one of the men responsible for collecting offerings and selling candles, and Mary was a member of the women's group, Srpska Zenska Zadruga. Natalie remembers the many hours and days that her mother worked to prepare for her family's Slava held each year on May 6, St. George's Day. Although Natalie no longer prepares a feast for this "important religious day for our family," she observes it each year. Mary's traditional Serbian kifle was served for the family Slava and most holidays, especially Easter and Christmas. *Contributed by Mary's daughter Natalie (Vukelich) Alexander.*

Kifle

Dough
1 cake yeast
1 pound margarine
6 cups all-purpose flour
3 eggs (1 whole and 2 yolks)
6 ounces (½ can) evaporated milk
Confectioners' sugar

Filling
½ pound finely ground walnuts
1 ¼ cups sugar
¼ teaspoon cinnamon
¼ cup butter, melted
½ teaspoon vanilla
¼ cup warm milk
3 egg whites

Dissolve yeast in ¼ cup lukewarm water. Cut margarine into flour with a pastry blender. Add egg and yolks to flour mixture. Add milk and yeast mixture. Mix thoroughly, forming a large ball. Knead on a floured board or counter until it is elastic and does not stick to the board or your hands. Roll dough into walnut-size balls. Chill in refrigerator for at least 2 hours.

Mix walnuts, sugar and cinnamon in a bowl. Mix melted butter, vanilla and milk and add to walnut mixture. Beat egg whites until stiff and fold into nut mixture.

On a board or counter dusted with confectioners' sugar, roll dough into circles about ⅛- to ¼-inch thick. Cut into 6 wedges. Place ½ teaspoon of filling at wide end and roll into a crescent shape. Place on greased and lightly floured cookie sheet. Bake at 375 degrees for about 20 minutes.

APPALACHIAN AND SOUTHERN

Haskell Jones of Mayfield, Kentucky, was one of thousands of young people who left Appalachia and the South for the promise of better wages and opportunities in the industrial North. In 1917, Haskell arrived in Akron on a train with other young men who had been recruited by what he described as "employment men," representatives of Akron's factories who went to small towns in West Virginia, Kentucky and other states to recruit workers for Akron's rubber factories, which could not hire them fast enough to fill all of the jobs needed to keep them humming around the clock. Haskell arrived with six dollars and no job or place to stay. He spent the first night with two others from the train in a flophouse. He tried to find a hotel room the next night but was told that there wasn't a room in town. He spent the night sitting in the hotel lobby. The next day, he ran into a friend, who helped him to get a job at Miller Rubber. From there, he took jobs with other factories, including Firestone and Goodyear, living in various rooming houses, most near to his workplace. Haskell's story, documented by his grandson Tom Jones through hundreds of hours of taped interviews and two books, is the story of thousands of young men and women who left their farms and families in the South. Many stayed and made a life for themselves here, forever changing the culture of our city. Some returned home permanently, while others moved back and forth, some due to layoffs and others because they were needed at home. Vacations or time off almost always involved a trip home. Life in the big city was not always easy for transplanted rural folks, and time with family in one's hometown was important.

WHERE THEY LIVED

Akron was booming, the factories never slept and housing for workers was in short supply. Many residents took in boarders, sometimes renting a room to three workers at a time. One would end his shift and climb into a bed that had barely cooled from his roommate, who was on his way to the next shift. Families with rooms to rent placed ads in the *Akron Beacon Journal* classifieds, enticing southern men with the promise of southern cooking and Sunday chicken dinners. One 1924 classified specified: "Rubber workers preferred, no foreigners, southern cooking, ten minutes to Goodrich." Some of the earliest recruits were relegated to sleeping in boxcars, chicken coops, shanties and event tents, according to a 1917 article in *McClure's Magazine* titled "Akron: Standing Room Only!" This article reported that women who came to Akron also faced housing difficulties, especially because most boardinghouses catered to men.

To house its growing workforce, Firestone and Goodyear created Firestone Park and Goodyear Heights, building modest homes that were affordable for the average worker. While many of Akron's southern transplants moved into these homes, a good number also settled in the neighborhoods in and around Ellet, Lakemore and Springfield Township.

CHURCH LIFE

While the social lives of Akron's immigrants centered mostly on their ethnic clubs, the anchor for Akron's southerners was church. They brought their religious traditions with them, establishing dozens of churches. By the 1920s, Akron had nearly fifty Baptist and Methodist churches, most of which were started by southern transplants. According to Steve Love and David Giffels's 1998 history of Akron's rubber industry, *Wheels of Fortune,* "some were Baptist, some were Pentecostal, some were 'shouting Methodists.'...The Southern religious folks celebrated with a fervor Akron had never seen."

Under the leadership of Kentuckian Dallas Billington, Akron Baptist Temple became one of the largest churches in the city. He came to Akron in 1925 and found a job with Goodyear, where he worked for eleven years. He struggled with what he perceived as Akron's depravity and in a letter to his young wife described Akron as "the wickedest place this side of hell." His concern was that his fellow southerners had drifted from their religious

Taken during a service celebrating the final payment of the Akron Baptist Temple's mortgage, this photograph shows Reverend Dallas Billington (at the microphone) and George Leonard of the Firestone Bank. *Akron–Summit County Public Library.*

upbringing because Akron didn't have any churches like those they knew from home. Soon he found himself preaching at the Furnace Street Mission and then in various churches in nearby cities. His weekly WJW radio station program drew thousands of listeners who were drawn to his message of the Bible. In 1934, he founded Akron Baptist Temple and was ordained a Southern Baptist minister. By the 1960s, his church boasted more than six thousand members, most of whom had southern roots.

The Chapel on Fir Hill, now known as the Chapel, was founded by Tennessean Carl Burnham, who began his ministry preaching at the Furnace Street Mission. Rex Humbard of Arkansas started his career as a traveling evangelist, later establishing the Cathedral of Tomorrow, one of America's first mega-churches, whose reach extended around the world by way of his television station. Another traveling evangelist who put down his roots in Akron was North Carolina–born Ernest Angley of Grace Cathedral. In addition to these large congregations, plenty of smaller churches emerged throughout the city to serve Akron's southerners.

CLUBS AND ORGANIZATIONS

As a whole, they were close-knit, establishing their own social clubs, including the West Virginia Society. *Rubber Age* magazine reported that one thousand former "Mountain Staters" attended the first meeting in 1916. During the society's heyday, tens of thousands of transplanted West Virginians attended its annual picnic, usually at Springfield Lake or Summit Beach Park. Because more than twenty-five thousand were expected at the 1929 picnic, posts were installed at Springfield Lake for each of West Virginia's fifty-five counties, ensuring that attendees could find "their people." Miss West Virginia was crowned, and prizes were given for the largest family and the best-looking couple. Some years featured hog-calling and homeliest person contests. Local, as well as West Virginia, politicians wouldn't miss these picnics. After all, West Virginians made up a large percentage of Akron's population, and many were still registered to vote in the Mountain State. By 1933, the West Virginia Society had its own building on South Arlington, the West Virginia Home and Hall, formerly the home of Akron clay industry pioneer George R. Hill. Members were assured that they could always find newspapers from West Virginia's largest cities. Although membership declined over the years, the group was still active into the 1990s, holding regular meetings and the occasional square dance. Sometime in the 1980s, the group published a community cookbook, *Our Favorite Recipes: Old and New.*

If you were from someplace other than West Virginia, you might have joined the Southern Society of Summit County. They too held annual picnics and social events. In 1935, members were invited to Summit Lake Park for an "old-fashioned basket picnic with fried chicken," where the speakers were Louisiana senator Huey Long and Ohio governor Martin L. Davey. Scheduled activities included a softball game between married and single men and a football-throwing contest for the ladies. Tennesseans had their club, too. The Tennessee Club held annual picnics starting in the 1930s, but membership had faded by 1970.

Akron's West Virginia Society was established in 1917. This annual event was enjoyed by thousands until the late 1970s. *From the* Akron Beacon Journal.

RESTAURANTS AND FOOD BUSINESSES

In addition to religion and music, they brought their food. "Southern cooking" meant more than fried chicken and cornbread, however. Foods and recipes of the South differed widely, and each region had its own food traditions dependent on what was grown or available. If you were poor, you cooked with ingredients that you could grow or raise or afford to buy. Southern food was mostly enjoyed at home; however, local restaurants catered to Akron's homesick transplants by offering Southern specialties, especially fried chicken. As early as 1918, the Red Cross Tea Room touted its southern-style chicken and hot biscuits. In the 1920s, Southern Barbecue on East Market was known for real southern barbecue, chicken and steak. O'Neil's department store advertised a Sunday chicken dinner special with southern-style cream gravy.

If you were looking for a home-cooked Southern dinner in the 1940s and 1950s, you could venture to Semler's Hotel in Cuyahoga Falls, which bragged that its new chef hailed from North Carolina, or even to the Zepp Club on Massillon Road, where dinners were served "Southern-style" while you enjoyed its floor shows. In 1950, Uncle John's Chicken

Cato "Smitty" and Nola Smith's Ira Avenue market specialized in southern grocery staples. *From the* Akron Beacon Journal.

House on George Washington Boulevard advertised a fried chicken dinner and dessert for a dollar. For fifty cents, Mills Tavern served up southern fried chicken dinners and homemade pie. Even the Resthaven Nursing Home on Diagonal Road advertised "country-like grounds and delicious Southern Style cooking and baking."

Smitty's Market on Ira Avenue was a destination for southern staples. For more than twenty years, Tennessean Cato "Smitty" Smith and his West Virginia–born wife, Nola, made regular trips down south for Lily White flour, smoked meats and other down-home favorites. Before opening Smitty's in 1994, they owned the Bellows Cash Market for forty-seven years.

Many Akronites with southern roots are only a generation or two removed from family who came to Akron for a better life and good jobs. Although southern accents are heard rarely these days and their clubs are long gone, the pride of these transplants and their descendants remains strong. They still go "back home," attend church with folks they grew up with and celebrate their heritage through family traditions, including fried chicken.

Good eatin', y'all!

OVA (MARTIN) MORRIS

My grandfather Dewitt Morris was born in Calhoun, Kentucky, in 1891. He was one of twelve children raised on the family farm. After serving in the army during World War I, he returned home and started courting my grandmother Ova Martin of Butler County, Kentucky. Instead of reenlisting after the war, he was lured by the news of jobs in Akron. He drove to Akron, took a job with Goodyear, married Ova and brought her to Akron, where their three children were born. In the 1930s, they bought a farm in Green. My grandfather kept his job with Goodyear, all the while running the farm and doing woodworking. My grandmother made a farmer's breakfast for him every morning at 3:00 a.m. (My mother, Ruth, who was the youngest, got up every morning to have breakfast then go back to bed until time for school.) During the day, she worked on the farm, canned, sewed and knitted clothes for her large family, and every evening she knitted, quilted and tatted doilies. In the 1930s, she made pies for Kresge's from fruit grown on their farm. Because she didn't drive, the company sent a car each day to pick up her pies, which became so popular that they started selling her pies whole for customers to take home. During the Depression, she always had enough food for the homeless who stopped by the farm—no one was ever turned away. During World War II, she joined the war effort and worked for Goodyear. She was an amazing cook and was able to take whatever was on hand to make a delicious meal. This Apple Nut Salad is a favorite of my family. It is served for Thanksgiving, Christmas and all fall celebrations. Contributed by Ova's granddaughter Marilyn (Burchett) Croskey.

Apple Nut Salad

Dressing
1 egg
1 cup sugar
3 tablespoons flour
½ cup water
¼ cup vinegar
Pinch of salt

Salad

5 apples, cored and diced. For the best flavor, use a variety (crispy, sweet, tart)
1 cup diced celery
1 cup chopped walnuts (We use pecans today, but they were not readily available when my grandmother made this)
Raisins or grapes (optional)

Mix dressing ingredients in a small saucepan until there are no lumps. Bring to boil, stirring constantly, until it thickens, and the flour is cooked. Refrigerate overnight.

Combine apples, celery, nuts and, if desired, raisins or grapes with dressing. Refrigerate. Serve the same day.

Patricia "Pat" (Steerman) Armstrong

Pat was born in 1930 in Belington, West Virginia, and moved with her parents, Edward and Hannah Steerman, to Akron when she was just six weeks old. Her father worked for Goodyear until he was laid off, sometime in the 1940s. He was briefly employed by the WPA, later taking on other work. One of her earliest memories is the day her father rushed home because her baby brother was sick. He was always clean when he came home from the mill room at Goodyear, but this day he was covered in what she described as something that looked like flour. In 1951, Pat married Thomas Armstrong, son of Tennessee native Edgar and Margaret (Rhoades) Armstrong of Kentucky, who came to Akron soon after marrying. Pat has fond memories of her mother-in-law's cooking, especially her "incredible" biscuits that were used for communion at East Market Street Church of Christ, where she had perfect Sunday attendance for thirty-one years. Younger members of the church, especially those who had been out the night before, looked forward to her communion biscuits, often snitching a bigger piece. Margaret's cranberry salad is a favorite of Pat's family and a staple at Thanksgiving, Christmas and even Easter, if she has any berries left in her freezer. She still grinds them with an old-fashioned hand grinder.

Cranberry Salad

1 bag fresh cranberries
2 oranges

2 apples
1 cup sugar
1 can (8 ounces) crushed pineapple
½ to ¾ cup pecans, chopped (optional)
3 (3-ounce) packages raspberry gelatin
2 ½ cups boiling water

Using a hand grinder or food processor, grind cranberries, oranges and apples. Add sugar and pineapple and mix well. Add pecans if desired.

Dissolve gelatin in boiling water. Add cranberry mixture. Pour into a mold or 9 × 13 glass dish. Chill in refrigerator until set.

Elmer and Alice (Endinger) Bard

Born in Hopkinsville, Kentucky, Elmer Bard came to Akron in 1917 as a small boy with his parents, Charles, a carpenter, and Mary (Powell) Bard. He met Barberton native Alice Endinger at Kenmore High School, and they married in 1934. As a young man, he worked in the family business, C.W. Bard and Sons House Wrecking, later working as a route driver for Castle Music Company, servicing vending machines and music boxes. After Elmer retired from Ernest Alessio Construction, they moved to Eustis, Florida. In the 1940s, Elmer and Alice owned and operated Elmer's Sandwich Shoppe located at 987 Kenmore Boulevard. Their daughter, Janis, remembered,

> *My parents divided their hours at work—with my mom working days because my dad didn't have enough patience to work with the students from the high school who came in for lunch. I can remember my mom being so proud that their restaurant was one of the few places where students were allowed by the school to enter at lunchtime. My dad worked nights because he was better able to work with the people who came in the evenings, many from the local bars. Their specialties were hamburgers and chili mac and cheese.*

Contributed by Elmer and Alice's daughter, Janis (Bard) May.

Elmer's Sandwich Shoppe's Chili Mac with Cheese

½ cup chopped onion
2 tablespoons oil
1 pound ground beef
2 cloves garlic, minced
1 (14½-ounce) can diced tomatoes, undrained
1 (14½-ounce) can tomato sauce
3 tablespoons chili powder
½ teaspoon cumin
½ teaspoon oregano
½ teaspoon paprika
1 teaspoon salt
¼ teaspoon pepper
½ teaspoon granulated sugar
2 (15-ounce) cans red kidney beans, drained
1 pound elbow macaroni, cooked according to package directions
Colby or Cheddar cheese, shredded

Sauté onion in oil. Add ground beef and garlic. Cook until beef is browned. Drain excess grease. Stir in tomatoes and tomato sauce. Add seasonings and sugar.

Simmer for about 2 hours, adding kidney beans 30 minutes before serving. Serve with cooked macaroni and top with grated cheese.

Mary Alice (Griffis) James

In the late 1930s, Mary Alice Griffis left the family cotton farm in Louisiana to join her older sister Angie and Angie's husband, who came to Akron in 1929 seeking work in Akron's rubber industry. Mary Alice never found a job in the rubber industry, however, and worked as a waitress and beautician in downtown Akron. In 1942, she married Mississippian Luther James. Mary Alice and Luther raised their three children on southern fare, including Sunday fried chicken dinners. In true southern tradition, Sunday dinner was served at noon after the family returned from church at West Hill Baptist Church. It was always served with mashed potatoes, lima beans swimming in butter and a simple green salad. Corn on the cob and sliced tomatoes were a summer addition, and a pitcher of sweet tea could be found on her countertop year-round. Although she never wrote this recipe down, her daughter Jennell Woodard learned to re-create it, using the same pot her mother used on countless Sundays. *Contributed by Mary Alice's daughter, Jennell (James) Woodard.*

Nama's Southern Fried Chicken

1 frying chicken, cut up, or selected chicken pieces with skin. Cut breasts in half.
1 tablespoon salt
1 quart vegetable oil
2 cups all-purpose flour

Rub chicken pieces with salt. Place in a covered container and refrigerate overnight. Remove chicken from refrigerator 1 hour before cooking.

In a Dutch oven or deep pot, heat oil to 350 degrees. While oil is heating, dredge chicken pieces in flour. Add floured chicken pieces to hot oil. Do not crowd pieces, and make sure that they are completely submerged in oil. Cover pot and cook, turning pieces once or twice, 20 to 25 minutes. Remove from oil with tongs and drain on paper towels.

Opal Hillyard-Wagner

Sixteen-year-old Opal Hillyard Wagner and her new husband, eighteen-year-old Austin "Bill" Wagner, arrived in Akron on September 18, 1948, the day after they were married in Barbour County, West Virginia. Bill had a job waiting for him in Barberton, but the young couple had no car and had to hitch a ride to Akron with Bill's uncles, who had moved here in the 1930s. Bill later took a job with Goodyear, where he worked for twenty-eight years. The Sunday after they arrived, Bill's aunt decided that they needed to join a church and took them to the Akron Baptist Temple, where Opal taught Sunday school for thirty-six years. When they retired, Bill and Opal bought a forty-three-acre farm in Belington, West Virginia, not far from land that had been in Opal's family since 1843. Opal still lives in Belington but makes regular trips to Akron to visit her children and grandchildren. Some consider pepperoni rolls to be West Virginia's state food. This popular snack, found especially in the northern part of the state, originated with Italian immigrant coal miners who packed them for lunch. Opal's recipe first appeared in the West Virginia Society of Akron cookbook *Our Favorite Recipes: Old and New.* Her mother, Onie, made them for her coal miner husband, Walter, to pack in his lunch pail.

Pepperoni Rolls

1 package dry yeast
1 ½ cups warm milk
2 tablespoons shortening, melted
2 tablespoons sugar
1 beaten egg
1 teaspoon salt
4 cups flour
Pepperoni, sliced
Melted butter to brush on top

Dissolve yeast in warm milk. Combine milk mixture and shortening in a large bowl. Add sugar, egg and salt. Add flour, 1 cup at a time, until it can be kneaded without sticking to hands. Knead until smooth and elastic, about 8 minutes. Form into a ball and cover with plastic wrap. Set in a warm place for 1 hour. Shape into rolls, folding in the pepperoni. Let rise until doubled in size. Bake at 400 degrees for 15 to 20 minutes. Remove from oven and butter tops. Serve hot or cold.

Florence (Jones) Jones

Marjorie (Jones) Knapp was born in Akron to Haskell and Florence (Jones) Jones, natives of Graves County, Kentucky. In 1958, she was a new bride living in Winston-Salem, North Carolina. Faced with cooking for her husband, she turned to her regular source of advice, her mother. Letters to her mother were filled with requests for recipes, and Florence responded with instructions. In 1960, Marjorie and her husband moved to Florida, where she taught elementary school for thirty years. Marjorie has many of her mother's recipes written in Florence's hand. Lelah Jones is the great-granddaughter of Florence and Haskell. Although she was only four years old when Florence died, Lelah has a distinct memory of Florence instructing her how to use scissors. Lelah cherishes her great-grandmother's recipes. *Contributed by Florence's daughter Marjorie (Jones) Knapp and great-granddaughter Lelah Jones.*

Fried Corn

These instructions were taken directly from a letter from Florence to her daughter, Marjorie.

About the fried corn, take a sharp knife and cut the grains off about halfway to the cob and scrape the rest out in a bowl or pan. Put a skillet with grease, according to what you need for the amount of corn, on the stove. When it gets hot, put the corn in it and salt to taste. Don't let it get too hot as it burns easily. Stir often so it will not stick or burn. After it has cooked for about 8 or 10 minutes pour in hot water to finish it up, for what you would make, it would probably take about a cup full. Cook until it tastes done. If the corn is not sweet enough, add a little sugar. I use bacon grease if I have it, but if I don't I use lard. If you use lard, be sure it is good and hot before putting the corn in, and be sure to fry it until the lard taste is gone before adding water. If the corn is real young, I usually do not add water, as it is pretty watery anyway. I could show you a lot better than I can tell you if you were here, but maybe you can do by this. I know you remember how it looks, so that will help you judge the amount of water to use.

Nola (Smith) Smith

Nola was about three years old when she came to Akron from West Virginia with her parents, Ocie and Doris Smith. While riding the streetcar on her daily commute to her job at Ohio Bell, she met Cato "Smitty" Smith, a handsome young man from Tennessee. After a brief courtship, they married in 1946 and were blessed with a son and three daughters. Cato always wanted to be his own boss and soon bought the Bellows Cash Market, which he and Nola ran for forty-seven years. After "retiring" in 1994, they opened Smitty's, a small grocery and meat market on Ira Avenue that specialized in southern staples and cured meats. For years, Smitty and Nola made weekly trips to the wholesale produce market in Cleveland and monthly trips to

Atlanta to stock up on hard-to-come-by southern grocery staples. During the summer, they sold vegetables grown on their farm in Edinburg Township. Daughter Janelle recalled:

> *My dad had a genuine concern for his customers' ability to pay for their groceries. He allowed them to keep a tab until they received their paycheck so nobody would go without food. A hard worker, he spent six days a week in the store and then worked in the fields until dark. He suffered a major setback at age ninety-five when he suffered third-degree burns over 30 percent of his body and spent two months in the Akron Children's burn unit. Upon discharge, and against his doctor's advice, he went right back to work. He was still working at the age of one hundred when he was hospitalized and passed away. My mother, Nola, who still lives on the farm, continues to receive phone calls from their treasured customers.*

Contributed by Nola and Smitty's daughter Janelle (Smith) Pakan.

Southern Collard Greens

Collard greens
Smoked pork (You can use any smoked meat—skins, ham hocks, shanks, etc. The amount of meat depends on the amount of greens. Smitty always bought his pork from Pressler's Meats.)
1 medium onion, chopped

Wash, rinse and remove the thick veins from the greens and cut them into uniform pieces. Boil the meat in a covered pot in about 8 cups of water (once again it depends on the amount of greens) until it falls off the bone, about 45 to 60 minutes. Place collards and onion on top of the meat and cook greens to desired tenderness.

Arthur L. Bell Sr.

Arthur left his hometown of Lobelville, Tennessee, during the 1920s and found work as a calendar operator with Goodyear, where he worked for forty years. Soon after arriving, he found a room to rent from Lebanese immigrants Sam and Rose (Haddad) Boanny, whose young daughter, Sadie

Marie, caught his eye. Arthur and Sadie Marie married in 1929 and had a son, Arthur Jr., and daughter, Carol. According to granddaughter Linda (Edmunds) Berger,

Grampa was a jack of all trades. He was always fixing or building things, including the house where I lived with my parents, Carol (Bell) and Norman Edmunds, on Miller Lake in Portage Lakes. The house was a duplex with my grandparents in the downstairs unit and my family of seven upstairs. Grampa talked about his mother, Ida (Fuller) Bell, making cornpone, which we assumed was cornbread, a major ingredient in this recipe. According to my mother, Carol, it has been made for every Thanksgiving for more than eighty years. Although Great-Grandma Bell made it with bacon drippings, and my mother used melted Crisco, I use canola oil. Making a recipe that originated with our Tennessee family helps us feel close to them.

Contributed by Arthur's granddaughter Linda (Edmunds) Berger.

Thanksgiving Cornbread Dressing

Cornbread
2 cups yellow cornmeal
2 cups flour
2½ tablespoons baking powder
1 teaspoon salt
2 cups milk
2 eggs
½ cup canola oil

Dressing
1 pan cornbread, crumbled
16 pieces white or whole wheat bread, cubed and dried
8 large stalks celery, chopped (2 to 3 cups)
1 large onion, chopped (2½ to 3 cups)
¾ cup butter
4 cups chicken broth, or more
2 teaspoons pepper
3 tablespoons dried, homegrown or purchased sage, or more to taste

In a large bowl, combine cornmeal, flour, baking powder and salt. Add milk, eggs and oil and beat until fairly smooth, about 1 minute. Pour into a greased iron baking skillet.

Bake at 425 degrees for 20–23 minutess or until a wooden pick inserted in the center comes out clean.

Crumble the cornbread and white or wheat bread into a large bowl. Sauté celery and onion in butter and add to bread with chicken broth. (You may need a little more chicken broth. It's better if it's too moist than too dry. The uncooked dressing should be a little on the slushy side.) Add sage and pepper and mix thoroughly.

Place in a greased 9×13 baking pan and bake at 375 degrees for 15 minutes. Stir dressing from the sides of the pan into the rest so that it cooks uniformly. Recheck the seasonings, adding more if necessary. Bake until browned and the center has set, about 45 more minutes.

Alberta (Bosely) Bonner

Alberta and Charles "Gene," her husband of nearly seventy years, have known each other since they were children in Belington, West Virginia, where their fathers were members of the local fox-chasing club. Alberta's mother was protective of her three daughters and didn't approve of young ladies having boyfriends or dates. Although Alberta and Gene never went out on one date, they knew they were meant for each other. In January of their senior year of high school, they ran off to get married in Maryland. Soon after their graduation in June 1953, they left their hometown for Akron. Gene took a job with PPG in Barberton, where he had worked the summer before. He worked there until his retirement. Gene and Alberta's first apartment was two tiny rooms in a building on Howe Street that they rented for eight dollars a week. For years, they spent a good part of each summer in West Virginia on Alberta's family farm. Alberta is an accomplished seamstress, quilter and knitter and makes knitted baby hats and booties for preemies at Akron Children's Hospital. When Gene goes home to West Virginia to hunt squirrels, Alberta knows just how to cook them. Alberta and Gene have three children and four grandchildren.

Applesauce Pie

Alberta insists that grocery store applesauce will not work for this. The sauce must be thick, not runny. Be sure to use tart apples. According to Alberta, sweet apples "won't cook up smooth." She uses the Crisco shortening pie crust recipe for all of her pies.

Pie crust dough for double-crust pie
6 to 7 tart apples peeled and cut into chunks. Granny Smith work well.
¾ to 1 cup sugar
1 teaspoon cinnamon
¼ teaspoon nutmeg

Place apples in a saucepan with a little water. Cook over medium heat until smooth, stirring constantly. Add remaining ingredients. Fill prepared pie crust with mixture. Add top crust. Bake at 350 degrees for 35 minutes or until crust is golden brown.

Carrie (Ray) Williams

Sara Ray Roberts grew up in the North Georgia town of Bowman, where her parents, Carrie (Ray) of Greenville, South Carolina, and Guy Williams of Toccoa, Georgia, settled after marrying. According to their daughter, Sara, Carrie didn't know a thing about cooking and had to learn from Guy, who had once owned a restaurant. Carrie became a wonderful cook and "tremendous baker" whose cakes were in great demand in the tiny town of Bowman, which didn't have a bakery. She sold them to friends, charging barely enough to cover her costs, according to Guy. In the winter, she gave cakes as gifts, knowing that the recipients would share the bounty of their summer gardens with her. Carrie was also a part-time reporter and wrote stories, mostly social news, for the local paper. After Guy passed in 1976, she returned to Greenville until moving to Lake Township in 1992 to live with her daughter, Sara. At Sara's encouragement, Carrie wrote down many of her recipes to create a cookbook for family members. Sara put it together and printed enough copies for their family but soon had to print more to meet the demand of everyone who requested a copy. Caramel cake is a traditional southern dessert and a favorite of Guy's. In 2007, Sara and her family held a party in honor of what would have been Guy's one-hundredth birthday. There was no question what the dessert would be. *Submitted by Carrie's daughter, Sara Ray Roberts.*

Southern Caramel Cake

Cake
1 cup butter, softened
2 cups sugar
4 eggs
3 cups self-rising flour
1 cup buttermilk
2 teaspoons vanilla

Icing
2 cups sugar
1 cup buttermilk
½ cup vegetable shortening
½ cup butter, softened
1 teaspoon baking soda

Beat butter until light. Add sugar and beat for 5 more minutes. Add eggs, one at a time, mixing well after each addition. Alternately, add flour and buttermilk, beginning and ending with flour. Mix well after each addition. Beat in vanilla.

Divide batter among three greased (and optional parchment paper–lined) 9-inch cake pans. Bake at 350 degrees for 25 to 30 minutes or until set.

Remove from oven and set pans on cooling racks. After 10 minutes, turn cakes out of pans onto cooling racks and allow to cool completely before icing.

Mix icing ingredients in a large cast-iron Dutch oven. Swirl in pan and keep ingredients moving. Using a candy thermometer, cook to soft-ball stage, 235 to 245 degrees. Remove from heat and beat with a wooden spoon until creamy and ready to spread.

Ethel (Ramsey) Casteel

My grandmother Ethel (Ramsey) Casteel was born in 1906 in Dungannon, Virginia, near the Tennessee border. She and my grandfather, Omar, from Coeburn, Virginia, and their five children moved to Akron after the end of World War II, looking for a better life. My grandfather found work at Firestone, which was quite a step up from the struggle he and his family experienced in rural Virginia. There was never enough money, but my grandma was said to be a legendary talent in the kitchen. She could make whatever the men hunted or fished taste delicious. This is her most famous dessert treat, which my family serves for all big gatherings, especially in the summer. But don't ever call it prune cake around the children, or they won't eat it. Just call it spice cake! Contributed by Ethel's granddaughter Karen (Casteel) Larson.

Prune (Spice) Cake

Cake
1 cup prunes, chopped
2 cups flour
1 teaspoon cinnamon
1 teaspoon allspice
1 teaspoon cloves
1 teaspoon baking soda
1 ½ cups sugar
1 cup vegetable oil
3 eggs
1 cup buttermilk
1 teaspoon vanilla
1 cup chopped pecans

Sauce
1 cup sugar
½ cup buttermilk
½ teaspoon baking soda
2 teaspoons light Karo syrup
1 teaspoon vanilla
1 stick butter, softened

Place prunes in a small saucepan. Cover with water, boil for 15 minutes. Drain and set aside. Sift flour, spices and baking soda together and set aside. Mix sugar into oil and beat until light. Add eggs and mix well. Add buttermilk, vanilla and prunes. Add dry ingredients, one-fourth at a time. Stir in pecans.

Bake in greased 9 × 11 baking pan for 1 hour at 300 degrees.

Put sauce ingredients in a saucepan and bring to a boil. Boil sauce 1 minute without stirring, Prick cake top with fork or a small dowel and pour sauce over hot cake as soon as it comes out of the oven. Let the glaze soak into the cake for at least an hour before serving.

Joanne (Sheets) Cunningham

Candace Aspromatis's West Virginia roots are deep. Both sides of her family have lived in the Mountain State for several generations, some as early as the 1700s. Candace's father, Robert Cunningham, met Joanne Sheets in Joanne's hometown of Morgantown, where Bob was studying for his doctorate in chemistry at West Virginia University. They married in 1954 and moved the following year to Akron, where a research position with Goodyear was waiting for Bob. Joanne and Bob embraced their new hometown and were members of many civic groups, including the Summit County Historical Society, Progress Through Preservation and Stan Hywet. Bob had a special interest in Akron history and genealogy. Candace has dozens of family recipes from her grandmother Martha (Ross) Sheets and great-grandmother Grace (Heston) Ross. A special favorite is Grace's baked custard recipe. Candace's mother made it often, but Candace especially looked forward to eating it during yearly summer visits with her grandmother Martha, whose Morgantown home stood at the edge of town on the banks of the Monongahela River. Although she lived in the city, Martha always had a big garden and a chicken coop. Candace remembers gathering the eggs that her grandmother used in the baked custard. Written on the recipe card is a note penned by Martha: "You probably have this same recipe….It's the one mother always used….She makes it often for the grandchildren, as they get milk and eggs that way." Candace is proud of her West Virginia roots and visits with her daughter and granddaughters whenever she can. *Contributed by Joanne's daughter Candace (Cunningham) Aspromatis.*

Baked Custard

3 eggs
2 cups hot milk
⅓ cup sugar
Pinch salt
½ teaspoon vanilla extract
Nutmeg (optional)

Beat eggs slightly. Add milk and remaining ingredients. Pour into custard cups and sprinkle with nutmeg, if desired. Place cups in a pan of hot water, enough so the water comes up at least halfway to the top of the cups. Bake at 350 degrees for about 45 minutes, or until set.

Alma Ruth (Wade) Bond

Alma was a traditional southern cook. Her specialties were fried chicken, cornbread, biscuits, green beans with pork seasoning, coconut cake and blackberry cobbler. She was born on a farm in 1899 in western Kentucky, and her mother died shortly after her birth. Her widowed father placed her with family members until he remarried several years later. She married at sixteen and in the mid-1920s came to Akron with her husband, Derbert, and two sons. The rubber factories provided work and a better life than the farm. Alma devoted her energy to her family and her home. This is a classic recipe for chess pie. Southerners love sweets, and ingredients for chess pie were staples in every southern pantry, so a sweet dessert was only a few minutes away. A modern twist was using a Pet-Ritz pie crust, but a standard pastry crust was the original way the pie was made. *Contributed by Alma's granddaughter Jane Bond.*

Chess Pie

1 ½ cups sugar
3 eggs
1 ½ teaspoons vanilla extract
1 ½ teaspoons vinegar
¼ cup butter, melted

1 tablespoon cornmeal
Dash salt
1 prepared pie crust

Beat together sugar, eggs and vanilla. Stir in vinegar, butter, cornmeal and salt. Mix well. Pour into prepared pie crust in an 8-inch pie plate. Bake for 10 minutes at 350 degrees. Reduce heat to 200 degrees and bake until set and golden. Cool completely before serving.

SAUERKRAUT BALLS

IT'S AN AKRON THING

Posts about sauerkraut balls on the Akron Recipe Project Facebook page elicited more interest than any other topic. Clearly, we are passionate about our sauerkraut balls! Crunchy and savory, this deep-fried delicacy of sauerkraut and ground meats formed into bite-size balls has been served at Akron restaurants and cocktail parties since the 1950s. Although its provenance is uncertain, its place in our city's culinary narrative remains solid. The first mention of sauerkraut balls in the *Akron Beacon Journal* was a November 9, 1952 advertisement disguised as a news article, "Blowing Bubbles" by Nick Yanko, promoting his Highland Square Bubble Bar's nightly Cocktail Hour Club. He invited his patrons to join him and "the entire crowd of talkers and kidders" to "sit around, relax and sip, snack 'n' smoke while they talk about the day's business, politics and sports." Customers could enjoy their famous "King Size Cocktail" and a "delicious serving of hot sauerkraut balls."

The Bubble Bar advertisement was soon followed by more from Akron restaurants and taverns that boasted about their house-made versions, all of which were "the best." A 1959 article about Whitelaw Cafe's new chef Steve Novokovich, formerly employed by Iacomini's and the Embers restaurants, mentioned that he would be adding one of his specialties, sauerkraut balls, to the menu. Akronites had the opportunity to sample "the best" sauerkraut balls almost anywhere—John Bahas' Waterloo, Anthe's, Balaun's Fairlawn Village, Skyway, Gus' Chalet, Tangier, Amber Pub, Bavarian Haus, the Modern Café, Iacomini's, Yanko's and the Brown Derby. In 1962, the

Akron Beacon Journal reported that Iacomini's made 11,300 sauerkraut balls between Christmas and New Year's. Papa Joe's, operated by the Iacomini family, still serves them today.

In 2005, *Akron Beacon Journal* food writer Jane Snow interviewed several restaurant owners, each of whom provided the reason that their recipe could claim the title of "best." The Waterloo Restaurant, famous for its super-sized version, used smoked ham, while Anthe's incorporated trimmings from prime rib. Others used various combinations of ham, fresh pork and sometimes corned beef. According to Parris Girves, whose father, Gus, opened the first Brown Derby in 1941, the chef's secret was not to grind the sauerkraut too much so that each bite would include strands of savory kraut. Local restaurant owner Ken Stewart, who once worked for the Brown Derby, suggested that the local steakhouse chain popularized sauerkraut balls in the 1960s and 1970s when they were served complimentary during happy hour. No matter what the recipe, every Akronite has a favorite. Some eat them straight up, while others prefer cocktail, marinara, honey mustard or other dipping sauces.

THE EARLY HISTORY OF SAUERKRAUT BALLS IN NORTHEAST OHIO

Who made the first sauerkraut balls in northeast Ohio? Although they are more popular in Akron than any other city in Ohio, Cleveland might just have beaten Akron to the craze. Gruber's, a Cleveland restaurant, served them as early as the 1940s. Established in 1907 by Max Gruber, the popular restaurant known for its German fare was located in the Arcade on Superior Avenue. The restaurant relocated several times until moving to its final destination at Shaker Square. Opened by his sons Max Jr. and Roman, it was regarded as one of Cleveland's premier white-tablecloth establishments. Although the new location focused on continental cuisine, specifically French dishes, its faithful customers clamored for the sauerkraut balls served at their father's original restaurant. According to Roman's son, William Gruber, his frugal grandfather who never wasted anything worked with his chef to develop sauerkraut balls, grinding together leftover meat scraps, bread crumbs and sauerkraut. Although we don't know for certain who that chef was, former Hudsonite Rick Vogel believes that it might have been his father, Richard "Dick" Vogel, former chef and part-owner of Marcel's Restaurant in Cuyahoga Falls. The family story is that Dick got the recipe in the 1930s when he worked as a chef at the Ambassador Hotel in Washington, D.C., brought it with him to Ohio and introduced it at Gruber's, where he worked following World War II.

Another possible Gruber's-Akron connection is the Brown Derby. According to Parris Girves, son of founder Gus, the Brown Derby hired Gruber's head chef, Amerigo "Don" DiCarlo, in 1964, the same year the Gruber brothers sold their restaurant. Did he bring Gruber's sauerkraut ball recipe to the Brown Derby? The word about Gruber's delicious cocktail bites spread. *McCall's* magazine published the restaurant's original recipe, and when renowned food and restaurant critic Duncan Hines tried them in 1951, he asked Mr. Gruber for the recipe. It appeared in dozens of newspapers in Hines's syndicated column, "Adventures in Good Eating." Soon, sauerkraut balls could be found on the menus of scores of restaurants, especially in the Midwest. Tom Brown's Chicago restaurant the Coach Light was known for its version, which was similar to Gruber's. The Coach Light's recipe appeared in the February 1958 issue of *Gourmet* magazine and, in 1991, was selected for its fiftieth-anniversary issue as a top hors d'oeuvre.

BEYOND AKRON

The word soon extended beyond newspapers, magazines and the recipe files of local cooks. In September 1955, WAKR TV's Chef Lorenzo showed viewers how to make sauerkraut balls at home during his Acme Grocery Stores–sponsored cooking show. An Italian immigrant, Lorenzo Simonetti worked as a pastry chef at the Statler Hotel in Cleveland and the Netherland Plaza Hotel in Cincinnati before becoming one of northeast Ohio's first celebrity cooks. His granddaughter Anita Schreibman, the keeper of hundreds of his typed recipe cards, found his sauerkraut ball recipe dated Friday, September 23, 1955, which is identical to the Gruber's recipe.

In 1996, the same year sauerkraut balls were named Akron's official food, Robin Leach of the reality show *Lifestyles of the Rich and Famous* tasted his first at Ken Stewart's restaurant. "It's very, ah, Akron," he remarked. Food historians and authors Jane and Michael Stern came to Akron in 2006 for a speaking engagement at the Akron–Summit County Public Library and took some time for a food tour, including a visit to Al's Corner Restaurant in Barberton, Strickland's and Swenson's. Although they didn't have a chance to try a sauerkraut ball, it is included in their 2011 book *The Lexicon of Real American Food*, a compendium of regional foods and their stories, which elevated sauerkraut balls to national status. The book also includes the story of how Mayor Don Plusquellic sent a package of Akron classics such as Or Derv brand sauerkraut balls, Menches's hamburgers, West Point Market Killer Brownies and Diamond Grille steaks to Portland, Maine's mayor Jim Cohen after he lost a bet for whose team would win the 2006 AA Eastern League baseball championship. Mayor Plusquellic missed out on a basket of Maine lobsters but had the fun and pride of sharing Akron's official food, the humble but delicious sauerkraut ball.

Their most recent brush with fame was in 2016, when famed Cleveland-born chef and television celebrity Michael Symon prepared them on an episode of ABC's food and cooking show *The Chew*. As his dubious co-hosts looked on, he explained that this midwestern specialty "reigns supreme" during the holidays.

Although they are found outside of northeast Ohio, most served south of us include ingredients not usually found in the northern version—cream cheese and sausage, rather than fresh pork and/or ham. The first newspaper mention of sauerkraut balls in Cincinnati appeared in the January 31, 1959 edition of the *Cincinnati Enquirer*. Cincinnati's Hyde Park Tavern claimed to be "the original when it comes to serving Dutch hors d'oeuvres….People who eat them are saying that this new innovation is wonderful with beer, as a party snack or for appetizer with a meal." A handful of German-themed restaurants in Columbus serve them today, and "sauerkraut bällchen" may be found on the appetizer menu of the Munich-based beerhall chain Hofbräuhaus, which operates restaurants across the country. Ohio's oldest continuously operating restaurant, the Golden Lamb in Lebanon, is known for its golf ball–size version. They are a staple at German festivals, including the Oktoberfest held each year by the Germania Society of Cincinnati and the annual Sauerkraut Festival in Waynesville, Ohio. Are sauerkraut balls German? Although they do seem to be more popular in cities with a strong German heritage, a search of classic German cookbooks and newspapers revealed nothing that would hint at any German origin. An internet search for "sauerkraut bällchen" found two recipes on German websites: "American Deep Fried Sauerkraut Balls" and "Deep Fried Sauerkraut Meatballs." Both include sausage and cream cheese.

SAUERKRAUT BALLS AT HOME

As Akronites discovered sauerkraut balls at their favorite restaurants, home cooks were eager to prepare them in their own kitchens. Recipes were elusive, however, and even the *Akron Beacon Journal* struggled to find a recipe. In 1955, home economics writer Jean McGhie reported that the combined cookbook collections of the *Akron Beacon Journal* and the Akron Public Library did not include any recipes and put out a call to readers to share theirs. A month later, she reported that the mystery had been solved and recipes had been found for the "tasty hors d'oeuvres that are a conversation piece at every party." During the 1960s, *Akron Beacon Journal* food writer Polly Paffilas offered to mail recipes to readers for the price of a self-addressed stamped envelope. In 1970, Action Line, the paper's problem-solving column, mailed 550 copies of the original Brown Derby sauerkraut ball recipe to readers.

In later years, food writer Jane Snow regularly published recipes and articles featuring local restaurant owners and commercial producers who shared what they knew about Akron's iconic appetizer. It was Jane who initiated an *Akron Beacon Journal* readers' survey to name Akron's official food. Of one thousand reader responses, the sauerkraut ball rose to the top over local favorites Swenson's and Barberton chicken. In 1996, Jane officially proclaimed Akron the Sauerkraut Ball Capital of the World. Her 2003 article featuring "Akron's 10 Most Wanted Recipes" included Chef Dick Mansfield's recipe from the Bavarian Haus, the East Market Street German-themed restaurant, which closed in 1994. Although retired from the paper, Jane continues to share her love of all things related to food and Akron through her blog, *See Jane Cook: Food with Attitude*. At a reader's request, she shared the Bavarian Haus recipe for "the sauerkraut balls against which all others are measured."

READY-TO-EAT

As sauerkraut balls grew in popularity, local food companies began making and selling mass-produced versions to area restaurants. Gruber's sold theirs in the Cleveland area. Local grocery stores sold Brown Derby sauerkraut balls in the late 1970s and early 1980s. The *Akron Beacon Journal* includes advertisements for Brown Derby's heat-and-serve version, including a curious one featuring an attractive young woman with the statement, "In Sweden, we are not embarrassed to talk frankly about sauerkraut balls." Stouffer's

Top of the Town on the thirty-eighth floor of the Erieview Tower—one of Cleveland's swankiest restaurants in the 1960s and a favorite spot to impress a business client or celebrate a special occasion—had such popular sauerkraut balls that the frozen foods branch of the company produced them for retail sales. Chef Rohr's frozen German sauerkraut balls made in Massillon could also be purchased in local grocery store aisles in the 1960s and 1970s.

The prepared version that many revere as the quintessential Akron sauerkraut ball is Bunny B, available from local grocery stores and restaurants since 1964. The early history of Bunny B was murky, however, until former Akron deputy mayor and local historian Dave Lieberth's curiosity was piqued by a memory from his youth. He recalled that his aunt Josephine McCullough had a friend named Bunny who often brought sauerkraut balls to his aunt's house. He didn't know her last name, but his brother Joe remembered that her name was Bidinger. Dave followed up with his cousin, Josephine's daughter Margie, who remembered Bunny and her visits where she and her mother played cards and drank highballs. Although Dave was disappointed that Margie did not remember the sauerkraut balls, he was delighted when she called later that day to report that she had discovered in her mom's recipe box a handwritten card for "Bunny's Sauerkraut Balls."

But how did Bernadine "Bunny" Bidinger's recipe become the basis for today's Bunny B's, first made by Akron's Salem Potato Chip Company? Calls to family members of the company's founder, Kareem Thomas "K.T." Salem, revealed the answer. Earl Hatfield, the husband of K.T.'s daughter Donna, filled in some of the blanks, suggesting that Kathleen Salem, widow of K.T.'s son Gene, would have more information. It turned out that Bunny was a friend of her brother-in-law William "Uncle Bill" Salem. Sometime in the early 1960s, Bill brought the idea for mass-producing them to Gene Salem, K.T.'s son and vice president of the company. According to Kathleen, Gene was the idea guy, always coming up with plans for new business ventures. She teasingly called him the President of the Corporation of the Month Club. Kathleen also confirmed Dave Lieberth's claim that Bunny B was indeed Bernadine "Bunny" Bidinger.

By 1964, the Salem Potato Chip Company produced sauerkraut balls for grocery and commercial sales. Based on Bunny's recipe, its version consisted of a mix of picnic ham, beef and sauerkraut, coated with crushed cornflakes. Over the years, the recipe was adapted for commercial sales. Eventually, they made two versions, one for grocery stores and a smaller version with less expensive ingredients for restaurants. Although the Salem Potato Chip Company closed in 1982, Gene continued to make sauerkraut balls, as well as Bunny B bagged ice. In the early 1990s, Bunny B was purchased by local investors Menelaos "Mike" J. Pastis and Pete Rizopulos. According to Pete, Bunny B employees would move between the ice making and sauerkraut ball production, depending on the time of year, as both were mostly seasonal operations.

In 2005, Keith Kropp bought the company, changed the name to Or Derv Foods and expanded it to include several new products. Soon after, he moved the operation from Maple Street to Johnston Street. In 2013, several investors bought a large share of the company, and within a year, the company moved to a modern new facility at the city-owned Ascot Industrial Park.

In 2015, the corporate name changed to Ascot Valley Foods. In addition to the traditional Bunny B version, they also produce the "Connoisseur Sauerkraut Ball," their best-seller for the restaurant industry. According to a representative of the company, they produced nearly thirty-two million sauerkraut balls in 2021.

Whether we enjoy them at our favorite restaurant, heat up a pan full of Bunny B's or make our own, they remain, after more than fifty years, a staple of Akron restaurants, parties and holiday gatherings. But not everyone has enjoyed these perfect cocktail treats, especially folks who didn't grow up here. "What do you mean, you've never had a sauerkraut ball?" Isn't this our incredulous response to an outsider who has never tasted Akron's official food? We insist that they are perfectly delicious, maybe one of the best things you have ever tasted. "You must try them! You will love them—we all do!" It's true. No one loves them like we do. So what if they are "very Akron"? That's a good thing—a good and delicious thing.

Gruber's Sauerkraut Balls*

Courtesy of William Gruber, grandson of Max Gruber and son of Roman Gruber.

½ pound lean, boneless ham
½ pound lean, boneless pork
½ pound corned beef
1 medium onion
1 teaspoon parsley, minced
3 tablespoons vegetable shortening
2 cups flour, plus more for rolling balls
1 teaspoon dry mustard

1 teaspoon salt
2 cups milk
2 pounds sauerkraut, cooked and drained
2 eggs, slightly beaten
Dry bread crumbs

Put meats and onion through food grinder. Add parsley. Blend well and sauté in shortening until browned. Add flour, mustard, salt and milk. Blend and cook, stirring constantly until thick. Add sauerkraut and put entire mixture through food chopper. Mix thoroughly. Return to skillet. Cook, stirring constantly until very thick. Cool. Form into balls about the size of a walnut. Roll in flour. Dip in eggs and then roll in bread crumbs. Heat oil to 370 degrees. Fry balls until browned.

*This is the same recipe used by Chef Lorenzo for his 1955 WAKR Television radio program.

Bernadine "Bunny" Bidinger's Sauerkraut Balls
Courtesy of Dave Lieberth.

1 medium onion, finely chopped
3 tablespoons butter
1 cup cooked ham, finely chopped
1 cup corned beef, finely chopped
½ clove garlic, mashed
1½ cups flour, plus 6 tablespoons
1 egg, lightly beaten
2 cups sauerkraut, ground in food processor and thoroughly drained
Lawry's Seasoned Salt
Worcestershire sauce
1 tablespoon fresh parsley, finely chopped
½ cup beef stock
1 cup milk
2 to 3 cups dry bread crumbs
Vegetable oil for frying

Sauté onion in butter until cooked through. Add ham, corned beef and garlic. Heat mixture well. Stir in 6 tablespoons flour and egg. Continue to cook, stirring until well blended. Add sauerkraut, dash of Lawry's Seasoned Salt, dash of Worcestershire sauce, parsley and beef stock. Cook until mixture forms a thick paste. Spread mixture on platter to cool and chill well in refrigerator.

Shape mixture into 1-inch balls. Mix remaining flour and milk to create a batter. Dip balls into batter followed by bread crumbs. Fry balls in 375-degree vegetable oil until a rich brown color.

Chef Richard "Dick" Vogel's Sauerkraut Balls
Courtesy of Dick's son Rick Vogel.

Dick was the head chef and part-owner of Marcel's Restaurant in Cuyahoga Falls. This recipe was transcribed from his recipe cards now held by family members. According to his daughter Barbara Vogel Thiel, her father's recipe was the prototype for all the sauerkraut ball recipes that followed in Akron/Cleveland area restaurants in the 1940s, 1950s and 1960s. Dick told her that he got this recipe when he worked at the Ambassador Hotel in Washington, D.C., in the early 1930s and brought it back to Ohio, possibly at Gruber's in Cleveland.

½ pound boiling beef (stewing beef)
½ pound ham
1 large can sauerkraut, drained
Salt and pepper to taste
3 eggs
1½ cups cracker crumbs

Cook meats together until done. Add sauerkraut, salt and pepper. Grind fine. Add eggs and mix well. Roll into balls. Dredge balls in cracker crumbs and French fry.

Chef Dick Mansfield's Bavarian Haus Sauerkraut Balls

1¼ pounds ground ham
6 eggs
2¼ teaspoons granulated garlic or 1 teaspoon garlic powder
1 teaspoon black pepper

¾ teaspoon cayenne pepper
1 medium onion, minced fine
5 pounds sauerkraut, drained and chopped
4 to 6 cups flour
Flour for coating
1 egg beaten with 1 cup milk
Dry, unseasoned bread crumbs
Oil for deep-frying

In a very large bowl, combine ham, eggs, garlic, peppers and onion. Add sauerkraut and mix well with your hands. Add flour a little at a time, kneading until the mixture is smooth and can be shaped into soft balls. Use only enough flour to achieve the proper consistency. The mixture will be sticky.

Pull off chunks of the mixture and roll between your palms to make balls the size of a golf ball. Place on cookie sheets and freeze until firm, about 2 hours. While frozen, roll in the flour, then in the egg-milk mixture, then in the bread crumbs. Freeze again and transfer to plastic freezer bags until ready for use, or fry immediately.

To fry, heat oil to 375 degrees. Fry a few at a time (straight from freezer) until the coating is golden brown and a fork easily pierces to the center. If the oil is too hot, the outsides will burn before the insides thaw and cook.

The Original Brown Derby Sauerkraut Balls

½ pound lean beef
½ pound lean pork
½ pound corned beef
3 tablespoons vegetable oil, plus more for frying
1 medium onion, diced
1 teaspoon Tabasco sauce
1 teaspoon Worcestershire sauce
1 teaspoon salt
2 cups chicken stock
2 cups flour, plus more for rolling
2 pounds fresh-packed sauerkraut
2 eggs beaten with 1 cup milk
Dry bread crumbs

Grind meats through food chopper using medium blade. Sauté meat in 3 tablespoons of oil until brown. Add onion and cook until transparent. Add Tabasco, Worcestershire, salt and stock. Blend thoroughly and add flour, stirring constantly. Mix in sauerkraut. Put entire mixture through food chopper. Chill in refrigerator for about 2 hours.

Roll into 1-ounce balls. Roll in flour. Dip into egg mixture and then bread crumbs. For best results, roll the balls one day in advance. Deep fry in 350-degree oil until brown.

Brown Derby Sauerkraut Balls II

This recipe is for the version currently served at today's Brown Derby restaurants. Courtesy of Parris Girves and Girves Brown Derby.

2 (99-ounce) cans sauerkraut
6 Granny Smith apples, diced and sautéed
4 eggs
2 cups Dijon mustard
3 tablespoons parsley, minced
2 bunches of scallions, minced
½ cup honey
2 tablespoons Tabasco sauce
2 tablespoons Worcestershire sauce
2 tablespoons ground white pepper
2 cups dill pickles, diced
2½ pounds shredded pulled pork
2 tablespoons roasted garlic
Flour for dredging
Eggs
Panko

In a large colander, drain the sauerkraut of all excess liquid. Combine all ingredients besides the sauerkraut and mix thoroughly. Mix in the sauerkraut in three stages to assure flavor. Portion into 2-ounce balls. Bread balls using the standard breading procedure (flour, egg wash and panko).

Deep fry until brown. Makes 24 servings (3 per serving) of 2-ounce balls. It may be reduced for home use.

INDEX

ABOUT THE AUTHOR

A lifetime resident of Akron, Judy traces her Summit County roots to the early 1800s, when her German immigrant ancestors settled in what is now Coventry Township. She is a graduate of The Ohio State University, Kent State University School of Library and Information Science and the National Archives Modern Archives Institute. Judy retired from the Akron–Summit County Public Library after serving for more than thirty-five years as a reference librarian and manager of Special Collections, the library's local history and genealogy department. Her love of local history, family history and food was the inspiration for this book. She and her husband, Jeff, live in the heart of Akron in a neighborhood that was once home to many of Akron's earliest Irish immigrants.

Visit us at
www.historypress.com

Visit us at
www.historypress.com
....